GUIDE TO THE
COMPANIES
ACT 1989

A comprehensive analysis and interpretation of the

changes in company law brought about by

the Companies Act 1989

Ernst & Young

and

The Institute of Chartered Accountants of Scotland

KOGAN
PAGE

First published in 1989 by
Kogan Page Ltd
120 Pentonville Road, London N1 9JN
in association with Ernst & Young
and The Institute of Chartered Accountants of Scotland

Printed and bound in Great Britain by
Biddles Ltd, Guildford and Kings Lynn

British Library Cataloguing in Publication Data
Guide to the Companies Act 1989: a comprehensive analysis
    and interpretation of the changes brought about by the
    Companies Act 1989.
    1. Great Britain. Companies. Law
    I. Ernst & Young, Firm II. Institute of Chartered
    Accountants of Scotland
    344.106'66

ISBN 0-7494-0088-9

Preface

The Companies Act 1989 (the Act) received the Royal Assent on November 16, 1989. Whilst the main purpose of this new Act is to implement the EC Seventh and Eighth Company Law Directives, the Government has taken advantage of the opportunity to introduce a number of other significant changes in company legislation. Some of the provisions relating to fair trading and the Financial Services Act became effective on Royal Assent, whilst the rest of the Act will be brought into force piecemeal by commencement order.

The book aims to provide a comprehensive review of all the significant changes to the Companies Act 1985 and related companies legislation. However, since these changes cover such a broad spectrum of company law, few readers will require a detailed knowledge of all aspects of the new Act. Consequently, by both dealing with the Act under eight broad subject headings and through the use of executive summaries at the beginning of each chapter, the book enables readers to easily identify those provisions of the Act which are pertinent to their needs.

This book has been written by members of the Technical Services and Corporate Recovery Departments of Ernst & Young, in collaboration with the Institute of Chartered Accountants of Scotland. The principal authors were:

Jeremy Bassil

Alison Brown

Hedy Richards

James Robertson

The book also benefited from the comments and editorial assistance of Matthew Curtis, Mike Davies, Derek Foster, Jimmy Graham, Roger Housechild, Ron Paterson and Allister Wilson.

A specially constituted Editorial Panel of the Institute of Chartered Accountants of Scotland guided the project. Particular thanks are due to the members of the Panel for their advice on the overall presentation of the book, as well as for their diligence in providing detailed comments on various drafts of the chapters. The members of the Panel were as follows:

Aileen Beattie	The Institute of Chartered Accountants of Scotland
Brian Minto	James Murray & Co
David Mitchell	Ryder Manufacturing Company Ltd
Brian Spence	Spicer & Oppenheim
Ian Stevenson	Scott Oswald
Alasdair Young	The Institute of Chartered Accountants of Scotland.

London, November 1989   **Ernst & Young**

ERNST & YOUNG OFFICES IN THE UNITED KINGDOM

ABERDEEN
50 Huntly Street
Aberdeen AB9 1XN
0224 640033

BELFAST
Bedford House
16 Bedford Street
Belfast BT2 7DT
0232 246525

BIDEFORD
27 Bridgeland Street
Bideford EX39 2PZ
0237 471881

BIRMINGHAM
Windsor House
3 Temple Row
Birmingham B2 5LA
021 236 9151

BRADFORD
Clifton House
2 Clifton Villas
Bradford BD8 7DW
0274 498153

BRISTOL
One Bridewell Street
Bristol
BS1 2AA
0272 290808

CAMBRIDGE
Compass House
80 Newmarket Road
Cambridge CB5 8DZ
0223 461200

CARDIFF
Pendragon House
Fitzalan Court
Fitzalan Road
Cardiff CF2 1TF
0222 484641

COVENTRY
Queen's House
16 Queens Road
Coventry CV1 3EG
0203 550607

DUNDEE
City House
16 Overgate
Dundee DD1 9PN
0382 202561

EDINBURGH
39 Melville Street
Edinburgh EH3 7JL
031 226 4621

EXETER
Broadwalk House
Southernhay West
Exeter EX1 1LF
0392 433541

FORFAR
Manor Street
Forfar
Angus DD8 1EX
0307 62516

GLASGOW
George House
50 George Square
Glasgow G2 1RR
041 552 3456

HULL
PO Box 3
Lowgate House
Lowgate
Hull HU1 1JJ
0482 25531

INVERNESS
Moray House
16 Bank Street
Inverness IV1 1QY
0463 237581

IPSWICH
Queens House
Queen Street
Ipswich IP1 1SW
0473 217491

LEEDS
Barclays House
6 East Parade
Leeds LS1 1HA
0532 434844

LEICESTER
Provincial House
37 New Walk
Leicester LE1 6TU
0533 549818

LIVERPOOL
Silkhouse Court
Tithebarne Street
Liverpool L2 2LE
051 236 8214

LONDON
Becket House
1 Lambeth Palace Road
London SE1 7EU
01 928 2000

Rolls House
7 Rolls Buildings
Fetter Lane
London EC4A 1NH
01 831 7130

LUTON
65 Park Street
Luton LU1 3JX
0582 410011

MANCHESTER
Commercial Union House
Albert Square
Manchester M2 6LP
061 831 7854

MILTON KEYNES
380 Silbury Court
Silbury Boulevard
Central Milton Keynes
MK9 2AF
0908 672882

NEWCASTLE UPON TYNE
Norham House
12 New Bridge Street West
Newcastle Upon Tyne
NE1 8AD
091 2611063

NORWICH
Cambridge House
26 Tombland
Norwich NR3 1RH
0603 660482

NOTTINGHAM
10-12 The Ropewalk
Nottingham NG1 5DT
0602 411861

PERTH
2-4 Blackfriars Street
Perth PH1 5NB
0738 33551

PETERBOROUGH
New Priestgate House
57 Priestgate
Peterborough PE1 1JX
0733 60348

PLYMOUTH
St Andrew's Court
Notte Street
Plymouth PL1 2AH
0752 673567

READING
Kings Court
185 Kings Road
Reading
RG1 4EX
0734 593171

SHEFFIELD
Talbot Chambers
2-6 North Church Street
Sheffield S1 2DH
0742 752929

SOUTHAMPTON
Wessex House
19 Threefields Lane
Southampton SO1 1TW
0703 230230

SWINDON
Old Town Court
10-14 High Street
Swindon SN1 3EP
0793 618822

TELFORD
Brodie House
Town Centre
Telford TF3 4DR
0952 291575

TORQUAY
Commerce House
Abbey Road
Torquay TQ2 5RU
0803 213013

List of chapters

Detailed contents

Chapter 3 Groups and group account 39

Chapter 1

Overview

1   INTRODUCTION

This book provides a guide to the main changes in company law which have been brought about by the Companies Act 1989 ('the Act'). It deals with these changes under eight broad subject headings, rather than following the sequence of the legislation; however, the relevant sections of the Act can easily be traced using marginal references which run alongside the text. While the book summarises the main changes and comments on their practical implications, it does not cover every detailed provision in the statute, to which reference should be made for a definitive statement of the law.

The changes made by the Act cover a very broad spectrum and few readers will require a detailed knowledge of all of them. This chapter therefore takes the form of an overview of the Act to enable the reader to gain a general understanding of it and to locate more detailed coverage of items of particular interest.

The main reason for introducing the new Companies Act was to implement two EC company law Directives, both of which have to be incorporated into the legislation of member states and be in force by January 1, 1990. These are:

(a)   the Seventh Directive on consolidated accounts; and

(b)   the Eighth Directive on the regulation and qualification of auditors.

However, the Government has at the same time taken the opportunity to amend a wide range of legislation. This includes many parts of the Companies Act 1985 and also the Financial Services Act 1986, the Fair Trading Act 1973, the Insurance Companies Act 1982 and the Insolvency Act 1986.

There are a number of reasons for these further changes in the law. Firstly, there has been the furtherance of the Government's desire to help businesses, especially smaller ones, by cutting the burden of regulation. In 1985, the Department of Trade and Industry published a report, 'Burdens on business'. As a result, a working group of the Institute of Directors was set up; its recommendations form the basis of a series of deregulatory measures designed to simplify the procedures under which private companies operate.

Secondly, the Act implements the conclusions of reviews into the workings of specific aspects of company law. These include:

(a)   the review by Dr. Dan Prentice of the doctrine of *ultra vires*, published in 1986;

(b)   the review by Professor A. L. Diamond of security interests in property (registration of charges), published in 1989; and

(c)   the Dearing Report on the making of accounting standards, commissioned by the Consultative Committee of Accountancy Bodies, published in 1988.

Thirdly, there are the changes that have been made in order to remedy shortcomings in companies legislation. For example, the Financial Services Act 1986 has been effective since April 1988 and in that time some significant problems with its operation in practice have become apparent, and are dealt with in the Act. The law relating to company investigations has also been amended; a major reason for this is to introduce regulations relating to the investigation of overseas companies.

Finally, the opportunity has been taken to simplify and modernise the language of the 1985 Act and make it easier to use. This continues a process which began with the 1985 consolidation, without substantive amendment, of the previous Companies Acts. Certain provisions therefore appear rather different to their 1985 Act equivalents but are intended to be identical in effect. In addition, there are also a number of new sections giving indexes of defined expressions used in parts of the Act.

2   IMPLEMENTATION OF THE ACT AND APPLICATION TO NORTHERN IRELAND

Only a few sections of the Act came into force immediately on the Act receiving the Royal Assent on November 16, 1989; these are mainly concerned with mergers and with financial services and further details can be found in the relevant chapters. The remainder of the Act will be brought into effect by commencement orders. It is expected that the accounting provisions described in Chapters 2 and 3 will apply to accounting periods beginning on or after January 1, 1990.

The provisions of Part VII, which are discussed in Chapter 8, can be applied retrospectively by a court order to insolvency proceedings which began on or after December 22, 1988 and which involve a participator in a financial market .

Much of the proposed new Act will not apply automatically to Northern Ireland, or to companies registered or incorporated in Northern Ireland. Equivalent provisions covering many of the matters included in the Act (including those relating to accounts) will be brought in by an Order in Council under the Northern Ireland Act 1974. However, certain other parts of the Act will apply to Northern Ireland at the same time as they apply to Great Britain. In particular, the power to assist overseas regulatory authorities, the sections concerning mergers and related matters, amendments to the Financial Services Act 1986, and some of the sections relating to financial markets and insolvency will apply to Northern Ireland.

3   CONTENTS OF THE BOOK

The remainder of this book is organised as follows. A fuller outline of the changes made to the law is contained in the summary at the beginning of each chapter.

Chapter 2   Accounting and related matters

The previous legislation governing company accounts has been entirely redrafted. This chapter provides a guide to the resulting changes which, while not fundamental, are numerous, and affect many aspects of the preparation, publication and filing of company accounts.

Chapter 3   Groups and group accounts

This chapter describes the effects of implementing the EC Seventh Directive. These changes are far-reaching, and include detailed rules which determine the entities which are to be included in consolidated accounts and how they are to be accounted for.

Chapter 4   Company administration

This chapter deals with the wide range of measures brought in by the Act in relation to a company's constitution and its administration. The main areas covered are as follows:

(a)   the introduction of the so-called 'elective regime' for private companies;

(b)   the registration of company charges;

(c)   a modification of the basic duty to deliver annual returns and a simplification of the existing requirements as to their content;

(d)   changes to the doctrine of *ultra vires* as it applies to companies, their directors and members and the protection of third parties on entering into contracts with them; and

(e)   a variety of other measures, including changes to the limits for the disclosure of interests in shares of public companies, provisions which abolish the requirement to have a company seal and a revision of the financial assistance rules making it easier for companies to provide funds for the purpose of employee share ownership schemes.

Chapter 5   Auditors

This deals with Part II of the Act, which is concerned with the regulation and qualification of auditors. Principally, it introduces the EC Eighth Directive into UK legislation; the Government has also taken the opportunity to change some of the other aspects of the law relating to auditors and to partnerships.

In addition, legislation relating to the appointment, resignation and removal of auditors has been amended. Although much of this is a consequence of the introduction of the elective regime for small companies, the law has been redrafted and rationalised.

Chapter 6   Takeovers and mergers

This chapter covers the changes made to the Fair Trading Act 1973, dealing with the mechanisms for merger control exercised by the Office of Fair Trading and the Department of Trade and Industry.

Chapter 7   Investigations

This chapter deals with changes in the investigatory powers and procedures which have been established under a number of different statutes, and in particular with measures designed to facilitate international co-operation between regulatory authorities.

Chapter 8   Insolvency

This chapter deals with the major changes in the general law of insolvency where the insolvent person operates in a financial market. Procedures adopted by the markets for safeguarding the performance of bargains and dealing with the consequences of default will take priority over the exercise by licensed insolvency practitioners of their rights, powers and duties under the Insolvency Act 1986 or the Bankruptcy (Scotland) Act 1985.

Chapter 9   Financial services

This chapter deals with various amendments made to the Financial Services Act 1986 which are designed to establish a more coherent framework of regulation which will be easier for practitioners to understand and therefore to apply in practice.

Appendix 1   Table of derivations

The table shows the sources, where appropriate, of the sections in the Act. It shows which provisions have been amended and whether the amendments are substantive and refers to the place in the text where the issue is dealt with.

Appendix 2   Formats

This appendix gives the revised formats for balance sheet and profit and loss account for groups and for individual companies.

Appendix 3   Small and medium-sized groups

This Appendix gives a series of examples intended to illustrate the operation of the rules in section 13 of the Act which provides that small and medium-sized groups need not prepare consolidated accounts.

4   ABBREVIATIONS

B(S)A85	Bankruptcy (Scotland) Act 1985
BSA86	Building Societies Act 1986
CA	Companies Act
CACA	The Chartered Association of Certified Accountants
CDDA86	Company Directors Disqualification Act 1986
Ch	Chapter
ChA60	Charities Act 1960
CS(ID)A85	Company Securities (Insider Dealing) Act 1985
DGFT	Director General of Fair Trading
DTI	Department of Trade and Industry
EC	European Community
FSA86	Financial Services Act 1986
FTA73	Fair Trading Act 1973
IA86	Insolvency Act 1986
ICA82	Insurance Companies Act 1982
ICAEW	The Institute of Chartered Accountants in England and Wales
ICAI	The Institute of Chartered Accountants in Ireland
ICAS	The Institute of Chartered Accountants of Scotland
MMC	Monopolies and Mergers Commission
OFT	Office of Fair Trading
PPA75	Policyholders Protection Act 1975
R	Regulation
RCH	Recognised clearing house
rep	Replaced or repealed
RIE	Recognised investment exchange
RPB	Recognised professional body
RQB	Recognised qualifying body
RSB	Recognised supervisory body
S	Section
Sch	Schedule
SEC	Securities and Exchange Commission
SI	Statutory instrument
SIB	Securities and Investments Board
SRO	Self-regulating organisation
SSAP	Statement of Standard Accounting Practice
The Stock Exchange	The International Stock Exchange of Great Britain and Ireland Limited
the 1985 Act	Companies Act 1985
the Act	Companies Act 1989
TU	Trade union
TULRA74	Trade Union and Labour Relations Act 1974
UK	United Kingdom

5   KEY TO MARGINAL REFERENCES

Marginal references in plain text are to the sections and paragraphs of the Companies Act 1989 and to other legislation before amendment; those in italics refer to other Acts after amendment by the Companies Act 1989. Many marginal references therefore have two elements, that of the section or paragraph in the Act itself followed by the reference of the section as it has been amended or introduced into the appropriate legislation.

Sections and paragraphs in the Companies Act 1989 are not followed by any Act reference, nor are references to the amended 1985 Act; in all other cases the section or paragraph number is followed by the relevant abbreviation.

The abbreviations have been used as follows:

S114   Section 114 of the Companies Act 1989, which introduces the new section
S390B   390B into the Companies Act 1985.

S25(2)   Section 25(2) of the Companies Act 1989 and section 389(1)(a) and (5) of
(a)&(b)   the Companies Act 1985, which is replaced by the Act.
S389(1)
(a) & (5)
CA85 (rep)

6Sch11   Paragraph 6 of Schedule 11 to the Companies Act 1989.

R4SI1986/   Regulation 4 of Statutory Instrument 1986 number 1992.
1992

The section references have been taken from the version of the Bill presented to the House of Lords for their approval of Commons amendments, together with those amendments. A final version of the Act was not available at the time that this book went to print.

Chapter 2

Accounting and related matters

1   SUMMARY

This chapter deals with the changes made by the Act which will affect the accounts of individual companies as well as those of groups. Changes relating specifically to group accounts are dealt with in Chapter 3.

The changes discussed in this chapter cover a variety of different subjects and the reasons for making them are equally diverse, ranging from implementation of the Dearing Report recommendations to changes consequential on the implementation of the Seventh and Eighth Directives. A number of the changes are made as part of the Government's drive to lift burdens from businesses; these include provisions allowing listed companies to send summarised financial statements to shareholders not wishing to receive full statutory accounts and allowing the members of private companies to decide to dispense with the laying of accounts before a general meeting. The latter forms part of the changes made in introducing the elective regime for private companies (see Chapter 4).

The mechanism for effecting these changes has been to replace in their entirety the 1985 Act provisions relating to company accounts. A number of changes are made to the accounts disclosure requirements applying to all companies. The most significant are an extension of the requirements in relation to directors' emoluments, the abolition of the requirement to show the emoluments of higher paid employees and a power to introduce by statutory instrument a requirement for disclosure of fees paid to a company's auditors for services other than the audit.

2   FORM AND CONTENT OF ACCOUNTS

The main changes are as follows:

2.1   Directors' emoluments

The disclosure requirements for directors' emoluments are moved from Schedule 5 to Schedule 6 to the 1985 Act and the following changes are made:

(a)   'Golden hellos'

Disclosure will now be required of amounts paid to obtain the services of a director. Such payments have become increasingly popular in recent years. This is no doubt partly due to the fact that they have, until now, escaped disclosure as remuneration in accounts, although it was possible for such payments to come within the scope of the requirement to disclose contracts of the company in which a director has a material interest.

3Sch4
1(4)Partl
Sch6

(b)   Compensation and pension payments in kind

Benefits in kind are required to be included in directors' emoluments for their services, but the Act now extends this to two separate but related disclosure requirements. These are compensation for loss of office and pension payments. The nature of any such payments must be disclosed. For example, if a director receives a car as part of a compensation package then the value of the car should be included in the total amount disclosed for compensation payments and the accounts should disclose that this amount includes the value of a car.

3Sch4
7(4)&
8(3)Partl
Sch6

(c)   Payments to connected persons and to third parties

Payments made to 'connected persons' or a body corporate 'controlled' by a director are now required to be included in the aggregate figures disclosed for directors' fees, other emoluments, compensation for loss of office and pension payments. Such payments are also required to be included in the figures shown for chairman's emoluments, emoluments of the highest paid director and to be taken into account in the number of directors whose emoluments fall within each band of £5,000. 'Connected persons' and 'controlled' bodies corporate are as defined for the directors' loans legislation and include spouses, minor children, partners, certain trusts and bodies corporate in which a director has a significant (usually over 20%) holding. Previously such payments only came within the scope of the disclosure requirements if they were 'paid to or receivable by' the director. This would arise, for example, if the payment were channelled through a connected person but passed on to the director.

3Sch4
10(4)
&13(4)
Part I
Sch6

In addition, a new separate disclosure requirement is introduced for consideration paid to third parties for making available the services of a director. Such amounts are required to be shown in aggregate. Benefits in kind must be included and the

3Sch4
9Part I
Sch6

nature of any such benefits disclosed. 'Third parties' means persons other than group companies, connected persons or controlled bodies corporate. For example, this provision would be likely to be relevant if a person were on secondment from an unconnected organisation (such as a bank) as a director.

For many years, directors' emoluments, pensions paid to former directors and compensation for loss of office have included sums 'paid by or receivable from' any person. With the introduction of the new requirements to disclose payments to connected persons, controlled bodies corporate and third parties, certain indirect payments come within the scope of more than one disclosure requirement and therefore risk being double counted. This would happen, for example, if amounts paid for a director's services were paid to a controlled body corporate which later passed on the payment to the director. The Act makes it quite clear that it is not intended that there should be any double counting of the amount. *3Sch4 10(4) Part I Sch6*

2.2   Higher paid employees

The requirement to disclose the number of employees whose emoluments fall within each band of £5,000 exceeding £30,000 has been abolished. This requirement was included in Schedule 5 to the 1985 Act. Some of the contents of this Schedule have now been moved to Schedule 6 and the rest has been rationalised except for this particular requirement which has been dropped.

2.3   Loans, quasi-loans and other dealings in favour of directors

The rules governing disclosure of loans, quasi-loans and other dealings in favour of directors remain unchanged. These require, *inter alia*, disclosure of certain transactions entered into by subsidiaries of the reporting company. It should be noted that the term 'subsidiary' rather than 'subsidiary undertaking' applies in this context (see Chapter 3 at 2). This means, for example, that a loan by a subsidiary undertaking will only be disclosable if the undertaking is also a subsidiary (under the new definition of that term). The limits for permitted loans and similar transactions have been increased (see Chapter 4 at 6.9). *4Sch4 Part II Sch6*

2.4   Disclosure of non-audit fees paid to auditors

The existing disclosure requirement for auditors' remuneration has been repealed and replaced by a new provision. This requires disclosure of remuneration of the auditors 'in their capacity as such'. The old provision did not contain these words and was interpreted not to include amounts payable in respect of non-audit services. *S121 S390A*

The new provision is supplemented by a power to introduce, by statutory instrument, a requirement to disclose remuneration for non-audit services rendered by the reporting company's auditors or their 'associates' to the company or 'associated undertakings' of the company. 'Associates' and 'associated undertakings' are likely to be defined by the statutory instrument introducing this requirement. *S121 S390B*

2.5   Revaluation reserve

Changes have been made to the rules on the use of the revaluation reserve. These are discussed in Chapter 3 at 3.5.2; the intention of the changes is to prevent goodwill arising on consolidation from being written off against revaluation reserve. However, these changes also affect goodwill on the purchase of a business. Arguably, it would have been illegal prior to the Act to write off goodwill against revaluation reserve in the accounts of an individual company. This is because the Fourth Directive, which was implemented in the UK by the Companies Act 1981, does not permit such a treatment. The position was less clear with respect to goodwill arising on consolidation because it is the Seventh Directive, which is being implemented by the Act, which regulates treatment of this type of goodwill. The matter is now put beyond doubt in relation to both types of goodwill.

2.6   Deferred tax

The Act requires deferred tax balances to be disclosed separately from other provisions for taxation. Previously, only other provisions were required by statute to be disclosed. This brings the Act into line with SSAP 15 which already requires such disclosure, so this change will not affect existing practice.

8Sch1
47Sch4

2.7   Consistency of accounting policies

The Act requires accounting policies to be applied consistently *within the same accounts and* from one financial year to the next. The words in italics are new and reinforce the consistency concept of SSAP 2. Existing practice should not therefore be affected.

5Sch1
11Sch4

An equivalent requirement for banks and insurance companies and groups has been introduced for the first time into Schedule 9.

4Sch7
Part I
18A(1)
Sch9

3   SUMMARY FINANCIAL STATEMENTS

The section of the Act permitting listed companies to send summarised financial statements to shareholders not wishing to receive full statutory accounts leaves many of the details of implementation to be provided by statutory instrument. Separate provisions still remain dealing with publication of abridged (now referred to as non-statutory) accounts (see 7 below).

It should be emphasised that the section applies only to companies listed on The Stock Exchange and not to Unlisted Securities Market, Third Market or other public companies.

The Act contains only the following requirements as to the contents of a summary financial statement:

(a)   it must state that it is only a summary of information in the company's annual accounts and directors' report; *S15 S251 (4)(a)*

(b)   it must include a statement from the company's auditors of their opinion as to whether: *S15 S251 (4)(b)*

    (i)   it is consistent with the full accounts and directors' report; and

    (ii)   it complies with the requirements of the Act in relation to summary financial statements and the relevant regulations which are to be made by statutory instrument; and

(c)   it must state whether the audit report on the full accounts was qualified. If it was qualified, the report must be reproduced in full together with any further information necessary for an understanding of the qualification. If the audit report included a statement that the accounting records or returns were inadequate; or that the accounts did not agree with the records or returns; or that the auditors had failed to obtain all the information and explanations they required, then the statement must be reproduced in full. *S15 S251(4) (c)&(d)*

The meaning of 'consistent' in (b)(i) above is not defined. There are two different senses in which the word is used which could be relevant. Firstly, the meaning could be 'not inconsistent' which would be analogous with the requirement for auditors to report on anything in the directors' report which is inconsistent with the accounts. Secondly, it might refer to the figures being based on those which appear in the accounts. In fact, this requirement seems likely to encompass both of these meanings.

Apart from the above, the form and content of summary financial statements are not described in the Act; these matters will be determined by statutory instrument, as will the mechanism for determining whether a member wishes to receive full statutory accounts. *S15 S251(2) &(3)*

Consultations on the contents of the secondary legislation have recently taken place; the DTI issued a consultative document in August 1989. The Government intends to make the necessary regulations early in 1990 so that listed companies with December year ends will be able to send summary financial statements for the year ending December 31, 1989. This may indicate that other deregulatory measures in the Act are also likely to be implemented quickly. The main issues raised in the consultative document are discussed further below.

3.1   Mechanism for determining whether members wish to receive full accounts

The Government intends that, if a company decides to take advantage of the new provisions on summary financial statements, such statements will be sent to all shareholders together with reply-paid cards which can be used to request the full accounts. This means that shareholders will automatically receive summary statements unless they opt to receive full statutory accounts rather than the other way round.

Two alternative methods of implementing this are suggested in the consultative document:

(a)   in the first year of implementation, summary statements would be sent to all shareholders together with a reply-paid card for requesting the full accounts. Requests for full accounts which were received at least, say, ten days before the meeting at which the accounts were to be discussed would have to be met. Shareholders would have to be informed that in future they would receive only summary statements unless they returned the reply-paid cards. In future years, the system would be the same, except that full accounts would have to be sent to those shareholders who had requested them in the previous year. New shareholders would be sent the summary statement with reply-paid cards; or

(b)   a notice would be sent to all shareholders, informing them that in future they would receive only summary statements unless they returned an enclosed reply-paid card requesting the full accounts. After this, new shareholders would either be asked in advance whether they wished to receive the full accounts or they would be sent the full accounts in their first year as members, together with a reply-paid card for requesting the full accounts in future years.

The first alternative would allow companies to take advantage of summary financial statements at an earlier date. The same effect could be achieved under the second alternative if the implementing regulations were to recognise elections made by shareholders prior to their coming into force. This would mean companies would have to anticipate the regulations in respect of the questions to be asked of shareholders.

Under the first alternative, companies would not be allowed to presume that particular groups of shareholders, such as institutional shareholders, will request full accounts. This cannot be done because of the fundamental principle of company law that shareholders should be treated equally. It could result in large numbers of requests for full accounts having to be dealt with at short notice. In any event, this approach would delay the circulation of full accounts to those wishing to see them.

3.2   Form and content of summary financial statements

The consultative document suggests that it should be possible to fit a summary financial statement on to both sides of a sheet of A4 paper. It suggests three different forms of statement depending on whether the accounts are those of a banking company or group, an insurance company or group or neither of these. The contents suggested by the consultative document for companies and groups in industries other than banking or insurance are reproduced below to give an idea of the level of detail envisaged. It should be borne in mind that the statutory instrument could differ quite radically from what is shown below.

Table 2.1: Suggested minimum contents of summary financial statements

Only consolidated information need be given in the summary financial statements.

A   **Essential   items**

1.   Matters required by the Act - see 3 above.
2.   Fair review of the development of the business of the company and its subsidiaries during the financial year and of their position at the end of it.
3.   Particulars of any important events affecting the company or any of its subsidiaries which have occurred since the end of the financial year.
4.   Indication of likely future developments in the business of the company and its subsidiaries.
5.   Amounts extracted from the full profit and loss account and notes including at least:
         (a)   turnover
         (b)   income from associated undertakings (or share of profits less losses if the full accounts are consolidated)
         (c)   interest paid and received
         (d)   profit before tax
         (e)   tax
         (f)   extraordinary items
         (g)   tax on extraordinary items
         (h)   profit after tax and extraordinary items
         (i)   dividends paid and proposed
         (j)   directors' remuneration
6.   Amounts extracted from the full balance sheet including at least:
         (a)   fixed assets
         (b)   current assets
         (c)   creditors falling due within one year
         (d)   creditors falling due after more than one year
         (e)   provisions for liabilities and charges
         (f)   capital and reserves
7.   Comparative figures for the previous year.

B   **Desirable (but not essential) items (views are being sought as to whether these should be compulsory)**

1.   Names of all directors who served during the year.
2.   Names and countries of incorporation (if not the UK) of principal subsidiaries and associated undertakings.
3.   Indication of research and development activities (if any).
4.   Contingent liabilities.

5.   More detailed balance sheet information analysing certain of the figures in A.6 as follows:

    (a)   Fixed assets:
        (i)   intangible assets
        (ii)   tangible assets
        (iii)   investments
    (b)   Current assets:
        (i)   stocks
        (ii)   debtors
        (iii)   investments
        (iv)   cash at bank and in hand
    (c)   Capital and reserves:
        (i)   called up share capital
        (ii)   share premium account
        (iii)   revaluation reserve
        (iv)   other reserves
        (v)   profit and loss account

It is clear that the above gives virtually no explanation of the figures, even if items B.1 to B.5 are made compulsory. Unless the company chooses, there will be no explanation of the impact of important events on the figures: for example, the effect and treatment of business combinations; a description of extraordinary and exceptional items (exceptional items do not even have to be disclosed). No information on reserve movements is required, other than the profit and loss information listed in A.5 in the above table. Neither is there any requirement to explain the basis on which the figures have been computed, as accounting policies do not have to be disclosed. Companies will be free to provide additional information, including promotional material, provided it is made clear which information constitutes the summary financial statements.

If the intention to implement this section of the Act quickly is carried out, the requirements for summary financial statements will have to be changed shortly after implementation to reflect the changes to the accounting requirements which will be implemented later. For example, 'subsidiary undertakings' will need to be substituted for 'subsidiaries' (see Chapter 3 at 2) once that definition has been brought into effect (which is likely to be for financial years commencing on or after January 1, 1990). The requirements for the banking and insurance industries will need to be changed again later when the relevant directives are implemented (likely to be 1993 and 1995 respectively).

4   ACCOUNTING REFERENCE PERIODS AND FINANCIAL YEARS

Consultations took place during 1985 on the subject of accounting reference periods and the filing of accounts and annual returns. The purpose of the consultations was to identify opportunities for the simplification and modernisation of the existing procedures and for improving the information on public record. In relation to accounting reference periods and financial years, it became apparent that any significant simplification of the rules for determining and changing them would result in a loss of flexibility. As a result, the only substantive changes made to the existing rules are:

(a) the period allowed for newly incorporated companies to nominate an accounting reference period has been extended from six months to nine months from the date of incorporation; and

S3 S224(2)

(b) companies which are incorporated after the accounting provisions of the Act come into force and which fail to nominate a date will be assigned the last day of the month in which the anniversary of their incorporation falls. This replaces the existing default date of March 31 and will give a more even spread throughout the year of the workload of Companies House.

S3 S224(3)

In addition, new terminology is substituted for the old, i.e. 'parent undertaking' for 'holding company' and 'subsidiary undertaking' for 'subsidiary' (see Chapter 3 at 2.2 and 3). This is relevant in relation to alterations of accounting reference periods which, in some circumstances, can only be made if the intention of the change is to bring the year end of the company making the change into line with that of a parent company or subsidiary undertaking.

S3 S223(5), 225(2)(a) &(4)(a)

5   ANNUAL ACCOUNTS

5.1   Laying of accounts

The only substantive change made to the existing requirements for the laying of accounts is that private companies may decide by elective resolution (see Chapter 4 at 2.2) to dispense with the laying of accounts before the company in general meeting. Such an election becomes effective in relation to the accounts for the financial year in which it is made and, as with other types of elective resolution, remains in effect until either it is revoked or the company re-registers as a public company. When an election ceases to have effect, accounts must be laid before the general meeting for the financial year in which it ceases to have effect.

S16 S252(1), (2)&(4)

When an election is in force, accounts will still be required to be sent to members, debenture holders and others entitled to receive notice of general meetings and the filing requirements will be unaffected by the election. The accounts must be sent at least 28 days before the end of the filing period.

S16 S253 (1)(a)

As with all types of elective resolution, an election to dispense with the laying of accounts must be unanimous but may be revoked merely by an ordinary resolution. Whilst an election is in force, any member can require the accounts to be laid for a particular financial year. The same right is extended to auditors. The mechanism for giving effect to this is as follows:

(a)   when the accounts are sent out, each member must be sent a notice   S16
         informing him of his right to require the laying of accounts;   S253
                                                                              (1)(b)

(b)   within 28 days of the accounts being sent out, any member or auditor may   S16
         require the accounts to be laid before the company in general meeting by   S253(2)
         depositing a written notice at the registered office of the company; and

(c)   a meeting should be convened within 21 days of the date the notice is   S16
         deposited at the registered office. The meeting should be held within 28   S253
         days of the date of the notice convening it. If the directors fail to convene   (3)-(6)
         a meeting, the person who deposited the notice may do so and a different
         time limit applies in that the meeting must then be held within three
         months of the date the notice was deposited. Any resultant expenses
         incurred by the person who deposited the notice are recoverable from the
         company, which is required to recoup them from the remuneration of
         those directors responsible for the failure.

If a dividend is proposed and the accounts are qualified, the Act provides for the   S16
auditors' statement required by section 271(4) of the 1985 Act to be sent to   S252(3)
members and others with the accounts. No provision is made in relation to
subsequent dividends based on the same accounts so in some circumstances
companies will find it necessary to call a general meeting merely to lay the auditors'
statement before it.

5.2   Filing of accounts

The periods allowed for the delivery of accounts remain unchanged (except for a   13Sch10
minor relaxation in the case of the first accounting reference period of an oversea   702(3)
company) so that, at least for the time being, private companies will continue
generally to be allowed ten months from the end of their accounting reference
period and public companies seven months. The possibility of reducing the filing
periods was raised as part of the consultations referred to in 4 above. Opinion on
the matter was divided and, not surprisingly, users of accounts were inclined to
respond more favourably to the suggestion than preparers. Amongst those against
the suggestion, many felt that non-compliance would increase with little overall
improvement in the information available on public file.

The consultations took place at a time when the percentage of companies filing
their accounts within the required period was generally agreed to be too low. No
doubt, to an extent, consultees felt that the situation ought to be improved before
any further change was contemplated. Since the time of the consultations, a drive
to improve compliance has had a significant impact so it is perhaps not surprising
that the Government has expressed the intention of reducing the permitted filing
periods. It seems likely that this will be done in several stages, as it is considered
that a sudden radical change would be too burdensome.

Powers have been taken to effect the changes by statutory instrument and it seems likely that the first change will be to reduce the filing periods to six months for public companies and nine months for private companies. It is to be hoped that companies will be given time to get used to the new accounting requirements of the Act before any such changes are made. *S20 S257*

The existing criminal penalties for the company for failing to deliver accounts have been retained. Civil penalties, which have been included in the legislation since 1976 but never brought into effect because they were flawed, are being increased and it is intended to bring them into effect. The penalties, which may be recovered by the registrar, will depend on the length of time which has expired since the end of the period allowed for laying and delivering accounts and will be significantly higher for a public company than for a private company. For example, if the accounts are more than a year overdue the penalty is £1,000 for a private company and £5,000 for a public company. *S11 S242(2) &242A*

All copies of accounts filed at Companies House must, like all filed documents (see Chapter 4 at 6.2), now bear the company's registered number.

5.3 Approval and signing of accounts, directors' report and audit report

5.3.1 Directors' report

It is normal practice for the board of directors to approve the directors' report as well as the accounts and authorise either a director or the secretary to sign the directors' report. The Act formalises this practice. *S8 S234A*

Changes to the requirements for the content of the directors' report are discussed in 6 below.

5.3.2 Accounts

(a) Approval and signing of balance sheet

Approval of the accounts and signing of the company balance sheet by two directors is a long-established statutory requirement. The Act relaxes this so that in future the signature of one director will be sufficient. This should ease the logistics of finalising accounts for those companies which have experienced difficulties in finding two directors in the right place at the right time to sign the balance sheet. *S7 S233(1)*

(b) Approval of parent company profit and loss account when consolidated accounts are prepared

The Act introduces a new requirement for the parent company profit and loss account to be approved when consolidated accounts are prepared. This is discussed in Chapter 3 at 3.3.

5.3.3   Audit report

The Act makes it a legal requirement that the audit report filed with the registrar must state the names of the auditors and be signed by them. This does not require all copies of the report to be signed, although all copies laid before the company in general meeting or otherwise circulated, published or issued must state the names of the auditors. Until now there has been no such explicit statutory requirement although it has been universal practice to do so. *S9 S236 (1)-(3)*

5.4   Banks, insurance companies and shipping companies

The Fourth Directive exempted banks, insurance companies and certain shipping companies from its requirements. When it was implemented in 1981, therefore, the pre-existing Companies Act rules were retained for such companies so that the form and content of their accounts is governed by what is now Schedule 9 to the 1985 Act rather than Schedule 4 which applies to other companies. A number of minor changes have been made to the rules governing the accounts of these companies, known before the Act as 'special category companies' (for example, see 2.7 above).

The accounts must now state whether they are prepared under the exemptions for banks or for insurance companies. This was not previously a statutory requirement (only a statement that the accounts were special category accounts was required) although the information would generally be apparent from the accounts. *S18(1) S255(2)*

Changes affecting the directors' reports of banks and insurance companies are discussed at 6 below and those affecting the group accounts of banking and insurance groups are discussed in Chapter 3 at 4.3.

5.4.1   Ending of special category status for shipping companies

The exemption from the Fourth Directive for shipping companies only applied for a certain period. This period has now expired so the provisions allowing certain companies to prepare their accounts in accordance with Schedule 9 rather than Schedule 4 to the Act now make no reference to shipping companies. This is not expected to have a significant impact as few, if any, companies remain 'shipping companies' for this particular purpose. The Secretary of State's approval was required for a shipping company to be recognised as having special category status and there has been an effective moratorium on new approvals for some years. *S18(1) S255*

5.4.2   Banking partnerships

In future, partnerships which are authorised institutions under the Banking Act 1987 may become subject to the same accounting requirements as banking companies. The Act includes a provision allowing such a change to be made by statutory instrument. *S18(2) S255D*

6 CONTENT OF DIRECTORS' REPORT

The following changes are made to the required contents of directors' reports:

(a) a requirement is added that, if the company has paid for professional indemnity insurance for an officer or auditor, the directors' report must state this fact (see Chapter 4 at 6.8); *S137(2) 5ASch7*

(b) additional disclosures are required in respect of directors' interests in shares or debentures. Details of options (and other rights to subscribe for shares or debentures of group companies) granted or exercised must be given. The wording of this new requirement makes it clear that all options, whether to acquire or to subscribe, should be included in directors' interests in shares or debentures, which removes any doubt there may have been on this question; and *3Sch5 2BSch7*

(c) banks and insurance companies which prepare their accounts under Schedule 9 must now give the following information: *S18(1) &(5) S255C*

> (i) a fair review of the development of the business of the company and its subsidiary undertakings during the year and of their position at the end of it;
>
> (ii) particulars of any important post balance sheet events;
>
> (iii) an indication of likely future developments in the business of the company and of its subsidiaries; and
>
> (iv) an indication of the research and development activities (if any) of the group.
>
> As a consequence of the above, there is no longer a specific requirement to disclose any matters material for an appreciation of the company's affairs. Previously, only companies which prepared their accounts under Schedule 4 were required to give the information listed in (i) to (iv) above. It remains the case that a parent company of a banking or insurance group which is not itself a bank or insurance company is subject to the normal directors' report requirements rather than the requirements as adapted for banks and insurance companies.

In addition to the above, the terminology has been changed to refer, where relevant, to 'subsidiary undertakings' rather than 'subsidiaries' (see Chapter 3 at 2). An exception to this is that the terminology has not been changed in relation to the disclosure of directors' interests in shares. This means that a director's shareholding in a subsidiary undertaking is disclosable only if that subsidiary undertaking is also a subsidiary. *S8 S234*

7   PUBLICATION OF NON-STATUTORY ACCOUNTS

There are new statutory rules on the publication of abridged accounts. These are differently worded and use different terminology, for example 'non-statutory accounts' replaces 'abridged accounts'. The effect appears to be identical to the existing provisions except that a new requirement is introduced for non-statutory accounts to state whether the audit report on the statutory accounts contained a statement that the accounting records or returns were inadequate; or that the accounts did not agree with the records or returns; or that the auditors had not obtained all the information and explanations they considered necessary. Previously, the rules were interpreted by some as requiring such information only if it affected the truth and fairness of the accounts. *S10 S240 (3)(d)*

8   SMALL AND MEDIUM-SIZED COMPANIES

The Act makes some minor changes to the rules allowing small and medium-sized companies to file modified accounts while still preparing full statutory accounts for their shareholders. Different terminology is used; for example, the provisions no longer refer to 'modified accounts' and, in the case of small companies, this term is replaced by 'abbreviated balance sheet'. Companies belonging to groups which contain an authorised person under the FSA86 are added to the list of companies which may not file modified accounts. A change of detail is made to the exemptions for small companies: movements on fixed assets must be given for those fixed asset categories to which a letter or Roman numeral is assigned in the formats, i.e. for each of the headings 'intangible assets', 'tangible assets' and 'investments'. Previously, no fixed asset movements were required to be given. *S13(1) &(2) SS246& 247 Sch6 Sch8*

9   DORMANT COMPANIES

The rules permitting dormant companies to exempt themselves from the obligation to appoint auditors have been replaced. The wording of the replacement appears to have the same effect as the old wording except that companies that are authorised persons under the FSA86 are added to the types of company which cannot be exempt. *S14 S250 (2)(c)*

10   DEARING REPORT

In November 1987, the Consultative Committee of Accountancy Bodies appointed a Review Committee, under the chairmanship of Sir Ronald Dearing, to review and make recommendations on the making of accounting standards. It published its report (the Dearing Report) in November 1988, with some of its recommendations requiring changes to company law.

Statutory backing for accounting standards was considered but rejected because it would make standards too legalistic and difficult to change quickly in response to new developments. Instead, a lesser form of statutory support was recommended as follows:

(a)   in the case of all 'large companies' (which would include all public companies but only very large private companies), the directors should be required to state in the notes to the accounts whether or not they had been prepared in accordance with applicable accounting standards, drawing attention to material departures and explaining the reasons for them; and

(b)   there should be a statutory power for certain authorised bodies or the Secretary of State to apply to the courts for an order requiring the revision of accounts which do not give a true and fair view.

These recommendations have been taken up and are discussed further below.

Two further related recommendations were made which were not taken up as the Government considered that they came too close to giving statutory backing to accounting standards. These were that:

(a)   there should be a general presumption in any legal proceedings that all accounting standards will have the support of the courts. This would not apply if, in a particular instance, it could be demonstrated that, despite a material departure, the accounts give a true and fair view; and

(b)   if there were a material departure from an accounting standard, then the onus of proof should be on the party contending that the accounts do give a true and fair view to show that this is the case.

Other recommendations of the report related to the structure for standard setting and could have been implemented with varying degrees of statutory involvement. The approach adopted involves very little statutory involvement: there is a power to make grants to the proposed Financial Reporting Council, although the Act does not specifically refer to this body. *S19 S256(3)*

10.1   Requirement to state whether accounts comply with accounting standards

Accounts must state whether they have been prepared in accordance with applicable accounting standards and give details of, and the reasons for, any material departures. Small and medium-sized companies are exempt from this disclosure requirement. However, paragraph 8 of the explanatory foreword to accounting standards continues to apply to all companies. This goes further than the Act in that it requires disclosure of the financial effect of departures, unless this would be impracticable or misleading in the context of giving a true and fair view. An amendment which would have required such disclosure was tabled during the passage of the Act through Parliament but was rejected by the Government on the grounds that it came too close to giving statutory force to accounting standards. *7Sch1 36ASch4 S13(1) S246 (1)(a) 4Sch7 18BSch9*

10.2   Revision of defective accounts

The Act takes up the Dearing Committee recommendation that the Secretary of State or other authorised persons should be able to apply to the court for an order requiring the revision of defective accounts. Authorised persons for this purpose remain to be defined by statutory instrument but possible candidates include the proposed Financial Reporting Council and The Stock Exchange. Fears have been expressed that, if more than one person or body could take action, indecision might result as to which person or body should do so. This danger needs to be addressed in setting up the new structure. *S12 S245B (1)& 245C*

The Act also makes provisions designed to ensure that, whenever possible, accounts can be revised without the necessity for court action. This is done by:

(a)   providing a procedure for the voluntary revision of accounts. Where the accounts have already been laid before the members or delivered to the registrar, the revisions which may be made are confined to correcting the accounts to the extent that they do not comply with the Act and making any necessary consequential alterations. Certain details remain to be clarified by statutory instrument including: *S12 S245*

    (i)   the application of this provision to accounts which have already been revised;

    (ii)   the auditors' role in relation to the revised accounts;

    (iii)   the action to be taken in respect of summary financial statements (see 3 above) based on accounts which have subsequently been revised and, although not specifically mentioned in the Act, non-statutory accounts;

    (iv)   although not specifically mentioned in the Act, the effect of the revision of accounts on dividends and profit-related pay. Dividends which have not been paid should only be paid if they can be justified on the basis of the revised accounts. The position is more difficult for payments which have already been made: at the very least, it would be necessary for any resultant deficit to be made good before further dividends were paid; and

    (v)   although not specifically mentioned in the Act, publication of the fact that the accounts have been revised; and

(b)   providing a procedure for the Secretary of State to notify directors of apparent defects in accounts, thus giving them the opportunity either to revise the accounts or to explain why they believe no revision is required. This is done by serving a notice on the directors giving them a specified period of at least a month to respond. If the Secretary of State is not *S12 S245A* satisfied with the outcome, he may apply to the court for an order requiring the accounts to be revised. This procedure also applies to accounts which have already been revised. It does not allow for other authorised persons to serve statutory notices; presumably such persons would need to have their own procedures for following up apparent defects in accounts.

The Act makes the following provisions relating to the procedure for a court order requiring accounts to be revised: *S12 S245B (2)-(7)*

(a)   the applicant must notify the registrar of the proceedings and the matters at issue;

(b)   if the court orders revised accounts to be prepared, it may give such directions as it thinks fit as to matters surrounding the revision. This would include the auditing of the revised accounts, revision of summary financial statements and directors' reports and notification to persons likely to rely on the accounts. It might also address the position of dividends already paid (see (a)(iv) above);

(c)   if the court finds that the accounts did not comply with the Act, then the directors may be ordered to bear the expenses of the court order as well as those of the company in connection with the preparation of revised accounts. This applies to every director at the time the accounts were approved unless he can show that he took all reasonable steps to prevent their approval. The courts will consider whether the directors knew or ought to have known that the accounts did not comply with the Act and may order different directors to pay different amounts; and

(d)   the applicant must give the registrar a copy of the court order or notify the registrar that the application failed or was withdrawn.

This procedure applies equally to accounts which have already been revised.

Since accounts are required to give a true and fair view, the courts are likely to have to decide what this means. This means they will have to go beyond the provisions of the Act and consider SSAPs and generally accepted practice.

The new civil procedure described above will be complemented by a new criminal offence of approving accounts knowing that they do not comply with the Act or being reckless as to whether they comply. *S7 S233(5)*

Chapter 3

Groups and group accounts

1   SUMMARY

Member states are required to implement the EC Seventh Directive on consolidated accounts in time to apply it for financial years beginning on or after January 1, 1990. This is the main motivation for the changes being made by the Act to the law on groups and group accounts. However, the changes go beyond the minimum necessary to implement the Directive in that the Government has taken advantage of the opportunity to reduce the scope for off-balance sheet finance schemes. The main effect of this will be that some companies which are not subsidiaries under the present definition will require to be consolidated when the Act comes into effect. Vehicles other than companies, including certain partnerships and joint ventures, can also come within the consolidation requirement.

Two new exemptions from preparing group accounts are introduced. Small and medium-sized groups will be exempt and the present exemption for wholly-owned subsidiaries of bodies corporate incorporated in Great Britain is replaced by a new, wider exemption. This will exempt companies with a parent company incorporated in a member state from preparing group accounts but with the proviso that group accounts of the parent must be filed instead. These must comply with the Seventh Directive and, if necessary, they must be translated into English. Partially-owned subsidiaries will be included in this exemption, although minority shareholders will have the right to request the preparation of group accounts.

The Act requires group accounts to be in consolidated form. This reinforces SSAP 14. The effect of this is that other forms of group accounts may only be prepared in circumstances where consolidated accounts would not give a true and fair view. It remains possible to exclude subsidiaries from consolidation although the circumstances where this will be permitted are reduced. It is, for example, doubtful whether many groups will be able to continue excluding certain subsidiaries from consolidation on the grounds of dissimilar activities.

Apart from these changes, the impact of the Act on most groups will be relatively minor as, to a large extent, it codifies existing practice. This does not mean that the Act can be ignored since, at the very least, all groups will need to be aware of changes in the wording of the balance sheet and profit and loss account formats and note disclosure requirements. Other changes include a reduction in the scope for merger accounting and increased disclosure requirements in relation to acquisitions, mergers and goodwill. Additionally, companies with associated or related companies will need to be aware that the term 'related company' is being replaced by new terminology with a slightly different meaning.

The mechanism for effecting these changes has been to replace in their entirety the accounting provisions in the 1985 Act.

2   GROUPS

The Act introduces two main changes to the definition of a group. Firstly, the 1985 Act definitions of the terms 'holding company' and 'subsidiary' are replaced by two sets of definitions. One set uses the existing terms 'holding company' and 'subsidiary' and applies for general purposes. The other set uses the wider terms 'parent undertaking' and 'subsidiary undertaking' which will apply for accounting purposes only. It should be borne in mind that the general definition applies in relation to certain disclosure requirements e.g. loans by a 'subsidiary' to a director of its 'holding company'; directors' interests in shares of 'subsidiaries' (see Chapter 2 at 2.3 and 6).

As a result of the new definitions, certain entities which are not subsidiaries for general purposes will need to be consolidated. Also, while it is true that the new definitions reduce the scope for off-balance sheet finance, it is also true that certain companies previously defined as subsidiaries will no longer be defined as such, either for general or for consolidation purposes (see 2.3 below).

The second significant change to the definition of a group made by the Act is that references to 'shares in related companies' are replaced by 'participating interests' which has a similar but wider definition. A further term 'associated undertaking' is introduced to refer to an entity in which a group has a participating interest and over which it exercises a significant influence. Equity accounting must be used for associated undertakings in the consolidated accounts.

These new definitions and their effects are discussed in more detail below.

2.1   Holding company and subsidiary

The main changes made by the new definitions of 'holding company' and 'subsidiary' are as follows: S144(1) SS736(1)& 736A(3)

(a)   to replace the present criterion of ownership of the majority of equity with one of holding a majority of voting rights; and

(b)   to replace the present criterion of control of the composition of the board of directors with one which makes it clear that effective control will exist only where there is a right to appoint or remove directors having a majority of voting rights at meetings of the board, on all, or substantially all, matters.

Satisfaction of either of the above will create a holding company/subsidiary relationship. However, as is the case with the old definitions, board control will not create such a relationship unless the company having board control is a member of the company over which it has such control. A company will also be a subsidiary of another company which is a member of it and 'controls alone, pursuant to an agreement with other shareholders or members, a majority of the voting rights in it'. This reinforces condition (a) above. Sub-subsidiaries are also defined as subsidiaries, as at present.

The new definitions are accompanied by supplementary provisions which expand upon the construction of voting rights and on the notion of board control. The practical effects of the new definitions are discussed further in 2.3 below. *S144(1) S736A*

2.2   Parent undertaking and subsidiary undertaking

As already mentioned, the new definitions of 'parent undertaking' and 'subsidiary undertaking' apply for accounting purposes only. The use of the term 'undertaking' is one factor which makes the definitions wider than the general definition discussed above. This term is defined in such a way that unincorporated associations and partnerships, but apparently not trusts can come within the consolidation requirement. *S22 S259(1)*

This does not necessarily mean that off-balance sheet schemes involving the use of trusts will succeed. In the light of the Government's intention to reduce the scope for such schemes, it would seem reasonable to view any such scheme as inconsistent with the requirement to show a true and fair view and therefore necessitating a departure from the normal Companies Act requirements. This view is likely to be reinforced by a future accounting standard.

The definitions of 'parent undertaking' and 'subsidiary undertaking' reflect the change in emphasis in the general definitions from equity ownership to voting control. Any subsidiary will automatically be a subsidiary undertaking, but the following wider criteria are added to those which appear in the general definition:

(a)   regardless of whether any shares are held, an undertaking will be a subsidiary undertaking of another undertaking which has the right to exercise a dominant influence over it by virtue of provisions contained in its memorandum or articles or a control contract; and *S21(1) S258 (2)(c)*

(b)   an undertaking in which a participating interest (see 2.5 below) is held will be a subsidiary undertaking if: *S21(1) S258(4)*

     (i)   the investing undertaking *actually exercises a dominant influence* over it; or

    (ii)   the two undertakings are *managed on a unified basis.*

The above are to be found in the Seventh Directive as member state options and it is in implementing these that the Government has gone beyond the minimum necessary to implement the Seventh Directive in the hope of restricting opportunities for off-balance sheet finance schemes.

'Dominant influence' is defined for the purposes of (a) above as the right to give directions with respect to the operating and financial policies which the directors of the undertaking are obliged to comply with whether or not they are for its benefit. A 'control contract' means a contract in writing conferring such a right. It must be of a kind authorised by the constitution of the undertaking and be permitted by the law under which it is constituted.

*4(1)&(2)
Sch9
4(1)
&(2)
Sch10A*

However, the Act specifically states that the definition of 'dominant influence' discussed in the preceding paragraph is not to be read as affecting the construction of 'actually exercises a dominant influence' in (b) above. The term in this context is therefore left open to interpretation, as is 'managed on a unified basis'.

*4(3)Sch9
4(3)
Sch10A*

It is possible that guidance on interpretation will form part of a future accounting standard. Questions are already being discussed, including that of whether there can be more than one dominant influence over a single undertaking. Logically, there can be only one dominant influence but that raises further questions. For example, if two companies have a participating interest in an undertaking and one of them exercises a dominant influence, is it possible for the other company and the undertaking to be managed on a unified basis? If not, it is doubtful whether there is any distinction between 'dominant influence' and management on a 'unified basis' but, on the other hand, the use of the two terms in the Act suggests that there should be such a distinction. If so, should both companies consolidate the undertaking? Under the old definitions, it was possible for a company to be a subsidiary of two other companies (which were independent from each other). It is probably true to say that at least one party usually decided not to consolidate because of lack of effective control and perhaps this would apply in these circumstances.

It is also clear that too narrow an interpretation of 'managed on a unified basis' could result in a joint venture being a subsidiary undertaking of one of the parties to it merely because that party has agreed to be responsible for routine administration. Possibly, control at policy level should be the determining factor but should this be control over financial policies or over operating policies or both? Given that control over both is necessary where there is a control contract (see above), perhaps it should be both.

The new definitions are accompanied by a Schedule which expands upon the construction of terms used in the definitions, including voting rights, board control and, as mentioned above, 'dominant influence' in the first of the two contexts in which that expression is used.

*Sch9
Sch10A*

2.3   Practical effects of the new definitions

During consultations on the new definitions, fears were expressed that the new criterion in the definitions for accounting purposes of directing operating and financial policies would be too wide. For example, it was feared that certain large retailers might have to consolidate some of their suppliers. This does not appear to be the case because the right to direct operating and financial policies must derive from the memorandum, articles or a control contract. This means that the *effective* direction of operating and financial policies is not sufficient; there must be a *legal right* to direct them. Also, some commentators have called into question the legality in the UK of the type of arrangement discussed in 2.2 above under which directions must be followed even if not for the benefit of the undertaking.

The scope for off-balance sheet finance has been reduced by the closing of a number of popular loopholes, including the following:

(a)   under the old definitions, rights deriving from debentures were ignored. The right to appoint a director could therefore be attached to debentures. By this means, it was possible for one company to have effective board control over another without being its holding company. The new definitions, both for general and accounting purposes, do not exclude rights deriving from debentures held by a member of the company; S736 (4)(c) CA85 (rep)

(b)   under the old definitions, if two companies could appoint equal numbers of directors there would be no control over the composition of the board of directors. Effective control might very well exist in these circumstances if the directors appointed by one of the companies had more votes at board meetings than those appointed by the other (this might arise, for example, because one company appointed the chairman having a casting vote). The new definitions, both for general and accounting purposes, make it clear that it is the right to appoint directors having a majority of votes at board meetings that will create a holding company/subsidiary relationship; S736 (1)(a)(i) CA85 (rep) S144(1) S736A(3) 3Sch9 3Sch10A

(c)   the holding by a company of more than half in nominal value of the equity share capital of another company would, under the old definition, create a holding company/subsidiary relationship. Therefore, if a company could arrange for a third party to hold at least half of the nominal value of the equity it was possible to have effective control without the controlled company being a subsidiary. The shares held by the third party could be designed to come within the definition of equity share capital even though no real participation rights were attached to them. As a result of the replacement of the criterion of majority equity ownership with one of control over the majority of voting rights, there are no longer any references to equity share capital in the new definitions; SS736(1) (a)(ii) (rep)& 744 CA85

(d)   vehicles other than companies, such as partnerships and joint ventures, can   S22
        no longer be used to avoid the consolidation requirement. Such vehicles   S259
        will not be subsidiaries but can be subsidiary undertakings. This does not   (1)-(3)
        mean that genuine partnerships and joint ventures, which are not controlled
        by the 'parent', will come within the consolidation requirement. A
        partnership or joint venture will only be a subsidiary undertaking if another
        undertaking has rights which equate to rights which would make a
        company its subsidiary undertaking. The Act contains provisions
        explaining how to construe references to 'shares', 'directors',
        'memorandum of association' and other terms used in relation to
        companies in the context of undertakings other than companies; and

(e)   opportunities are reduced for using options over shares to delay   SS21(1)
        consolidation until a convenient time. Under the old definitions, options   &22
        were disregarded so consolidation could be delayed until their exercise.   SS258(4)
        The terms of the options could be designed to ensure their exercise before a   &260(3)
        particular point in time. For example, the eventual intended owner could
        have a call option (i.e. a right to buy the shares) exercisable at any time
        before a certain date whilst the temporary owner could have a put option
        (i.e. a right to sell the shares to the eventual intended owner) exercisable
        on or after that date at an unrealistically high price. Options come within
        the definition of 'participating interests'. A holding of options in an
        undertaking can therefore result in it being a subsidiary undertaking (but
        not a subsidiary) if 'dominant influence' is exercised or management is on
        a 'unified basis'. As discussed in 2.2 above, these terms are left open to
        interpretation.

The closing of the loopholes described above is likely eventually to be reinforced
by an accounting standard dealing with off-balance sheet finance.

The example below shows the effect of the new definitions on a typical off-balance
sheet finance scheme. It is a simplified version of one of the highly complex
schemes which are to be found in practice. The loopholes exploited by the scheme
in the example are described in (a) and (c) above.

Example 1   Effect of new definition on off-balance sheet finance scheme

The shares of S Limited, each of which has a nominal value of £1, are held as follows:

Class	Rights
Held by H Limited:	
100 Ordinary shares (the 'O shares')	Full voting rights, dividend rights and rights to share in surplus assets on winding up. Right to appoint one director.
800 B Preference shares (the 'B shares')	No voting rights, fixed dividend and no right to share in surplus assets on winding up.

Held by I Limited:
100 A Preference shares (the 'A shares')   Full voting rights, no dividend rights but
                                                            equal participation with the O shares on
                                                            winding up. Right to appoint one director.

In addition, S has outstanding debentures held by H which on winding up is repayable at such a premium as to absorb 99% of surplus assets and which gives H the right to appoint a further director.

H has effective control over S because, although H and I are entitled to appoint an equal number of directors under the rights granted by their shareholdings, H can appoint an extra director under the terms of the debentures giving it effective control over the board of S but:

(a)   is S a subsidiary of H under the old definition?

'Equity share capital' is defined as 'issued share capital excluding any part of that capital which, neither as respects dividends nor as respects capital, carries any right to participate beyond a specified amount in a distribution'. Under this definition, the O and the A shares are equity but the B shares are not. The A shares are equity because although they do not participate in profits they have the same participation as the O shares in surplus assets on winding up. Therefore H does not hold more than half in nominal value of the equity share capital of S. *S744 CA85*

H is not regarded as controlling the composition of the board of directors of S despite the effective control because the rights under the debentures are ignored for the purposes of the old definition. *S736 (4)(c) CA85 (rep)*

The conditions in subsection (1) of the old section 736 of the 1985 Act are therefore not satisfied so S is not a subsidiary of H under the old definition.

(b)   is S a subsidiary of H under the new definition?

H is a member of S and has the right to appoint or remove a majority of its board of directors. It is not relevant for the purposes of the new definition how the right to appoint or remove directors arises. S is therefore a subsidiary of H under the new definition. *S144(1) S736 (1)(b)*

(c)   is S a subsidiary undertaking of H?

The definition of 'subsidiary undertaking' contains identical conditions to those discussed under (b) above so S is a subsidiary undertaking of H. *S21(1) S258 (2)(b)*

Despite the significant widening of the consolidation requirement, the new definitions are narrower in that majority equity ownership will no longer of itself create a holding company/subsidiary relationship, nor will it of itself create a parent undertaking/subsidiary undertaking relationship. Companies in which a majority of equity is owned but over which there is no voting control (either through voting shares or by board control) will therefore no longer be subsidiaries and will not come within the consolidation requirement.

2.4   References to 'holding company' and 'subsidiary' in existing documents and legislation

Companies will need to consider references to 'holding company' and 'subsidiary'   S144(6)
in their articles, agreements and other documents to decide whether the reference
should be to the old definitions, the new definitions or the new definitions for
accounting purposes. The Act creates no presumption in relation to private
agreements, leaving them to be interpreted on an individual basis. This will not be
difficult where the agreement contains its own definition but frequently there will
be room for doubt. Therefore, where there are companies which are subsidiaries
under the new definition but not the old, or *vice versa*, it will often be necessary for
companies to consult their legal advisers on the construction of private agreements
and for suggestions as to how they ought to be amended. Variations will, of
course, require the consent of other parties to the agreement so this is a potential
source of discord and, possibly, litigation.

In relation to legislation, including subordinate legislation, the new definitions are   S144
generally substituted for the old.   (2)&(4)

The Act modifies enactments which use the terms 'holding company' or
'subsidiary'. The following points are worth noting:

(a)   a company which is a member of another company which becomes its   32Sch18
        holding company as a result of the new definition may continue to be a
        member but has no voting rights. This is consistent with new rules which
        replace the existing prohibition on subsidiaries being members of their
        holding companies (see Chapter 4 at 6.11);

(b)   if a company becomes a subsidiary of a public company as a result of the   34Sch18
        new definition, then the age limit for directors of public companies and their
        subsidiaries does not apply to directors of such subsidiaries who are already
        over 70 when the definition comes into force; and

(c)   an employees' share scheme in which a group company participates will   37Sch18
        not cease to be an employees' share scheme for Companies Act purposes
        solely because that company is no longer a subsidiary as a result of the
        new definition. The expression 'employees' share scheme' is used in the
        1985 Act in various sections dealing with share ownership, allotments of
        shares and transfers of shares. For example, as an exception to the general
        prohibition on the giving of financial assistance by a company for the
        purchase of its own shares, a company may give financial assistance to an
        employees' share scheme.

SSAP 14 includes a definition of 'subsidiary company' which is out of date in that
it refers to section 154 of the Companies Act 1948 (which became, without
modification, section 736 of the 1985 Act). The Accounting Standards Committee
is to revise the accounting standards which deal with group accounts and will no
doubt take into account the definition of subsidiary undertaking.

2.5   Associated undertakings and participating interests

As already mentioned, the term 'related company' is being replaced. Two new terms are introduced: 'participating interest' and 'associated undertaking'.

An investment by an individual undertaking which amounts to a participating interest is essentially the same as a related company. The main change that the Act makes is that 'participating interests' can include interests in undertakings which are not companies. Also, the holding of options or convertible loan stock can give rise to a participating interest. *S22 S260 92Sch4 CA85 (rep)*

In relation to group accounts, participating interests include interests held by all group companies. By contrast, in relation to the individual accounts of a company, only the interests of that company are taken into account. Arguably, the same was true of the definition of 'related company' because of the general rule that group accounts should comply with the statutory accounting requirements 'as if they were the accounts of an actual company.' The new provisions make this much clearer. *S22 S260(7) Formats &62(rep) Sch4 CA85*

Broadly, an 'associated undertaking' is an undertaking in which a participating interest is held and over which significant influence is exercised. This definition is much closer to that of 'associated company' than was the term 'related company'. It remains to be seen whether cases will emerge of associated companies which are not associated undertakings or *vice versa*. Such cases could give rise to the question of whether it is still legal to comply with SSAP 1 and equity account for an associated company which is not an associated undertaking. *20Sch2 20Sch4A*

Under SSAP 1, unincorporated joint ventures can fall to be treated as if they were associated companies. Where this happens, the joint venture is likely to be an associated undertaking. The Act allows proportional consolidation as an alternative to equity accounting in some such cases (see 3.5.6) and SSAP 1 acknowledges this as a possible treatment (see SSAP 1 paragraph 10). A joint venture which is proportionally consolidated is excluded from the definition of 'associated undertaking'.

The decision chart which follows on page 48 illustrates the effects of the new statutory definitions.

The following changes are made to the statutory accounting requirements as a result of the definitions discussed above:

(a)   references to 'shares in related companies' in the balance sheet and profit and loss account formats in Schedule 4 are replaced by references to 'participating interests'; *3Sch1*

(b)   references to 'related companies' in Schedule 4 are replaced by references to 'undertakings in which the company has a participating interest'; *4(1)Sch1 Formats Sch4*

Decision chart – participating interests and associated undertakings

A is a company and B an undertaking but not necessarily a company.

Participating interest – accounts of A

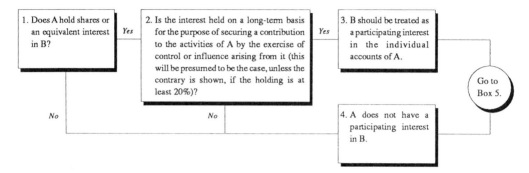

Participating interest – group accounts of A

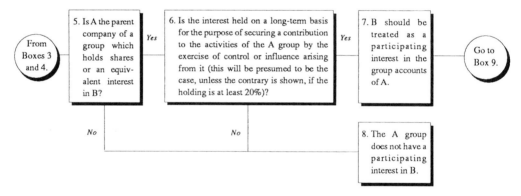

Associated undertaking

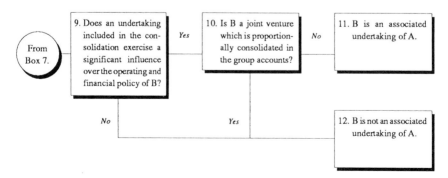

(c)   paragraph 65 of Schedule 4 to the 1985 Act has been repealed: this 22Sch2
22Sch4A *permitted* equity accounting in respect of companies (whether related companies or not) where a 'close association' existed. It has been replaced by a new provision *requiring* associated undertakings to be equity accounted. In practice, this is unlikely to have any significant effect on most groups where related companies and associated companies are one and the same thing and are accounted for using the equity method in accordance with SSAP 1; and

(d)   in relation to group accounts, the formats are adapted to split participating 21Sch2
21Sch4A interests into associated undertakings and other participating interests. Individual company accounts are not required to disclose associated undertakings separately. Investment companies may have participating interests which are not associated undertakings as they often have large holdings in other companies which are not treated as associated companies on the basis that there is no significant influence.

3   REQUIREMENT TO PREPARE GROUP ACCOUNTS

Group accounts must now be in consolidated form. Other forms of group accounts S5(1)
S227(2) may only be used if that is the only way to give a true and fair view. This means that the circumstances must be such that consolidated accounts would not show a true and fair view. This contrasts with previous Companies Acts which allowed other forms of group accounts in cases where the directors considered an alternative presentation would be more readily appreciated by members. The use of other forms is not common, as SSAP 14 generally requires group accounts to be in consolidated form.

As described in 2 above, the term 'subsidiary undertaking' has been introduced for S5(1)
S227(1) accounting purposes. Parent companies are, with certain exceptions, required to consolidate all subsidiary undertakings. A parent company means a parent undertaking which is a company, so the Act does not require entities other than companies to prepare consolidated accounts, although such a requirement could have been introduced under the Seventh Directive. By contrast, entities other than companies may need to be consolidated by a parent company (see 2.3(d)above).

3.1   Exemptions from preparing consolidated accounts

The Act introduces an exemption from preparing consolidated accounts for smaller groups. This is completely new to British law which until now has contained no such exemptions on grounds of size. The most useful exemption available before the Act was that wholly-owned subsidiaries of bodies corporate incorporated in

Great Britain were not required to prepare group accounts. This exemption has now been modified to exempt parent companies which have EC parents. The exemption is wider in that subsidiaries need not necessarily be wholly owned to claim it, but narrower in that only intermediate holding companies whose *immediate* parent is incorporated in a member state may claim it (see Example 2 in 3.1.2 below). Also, there is a new condition that a subsidiary claiming exemption must file an English translation of the accounts of an EC parent, which have been prepared under the Seventh Directive. This can lead to the same set of group accounts being filed by a number of companies, which seems unnecessarily bureaucratic but appears to be the literal requirement, although arguably not the intention, of the Seventh Directive.

In addition to the exemptions from preparing consolidated accounts, the Act sets out circumstances under which subsidiaries may be excluded from consolidation. If such circumstances apply to all the subsidiaries of a parent company, then consolidated accounts are not required. These exclusions are discussed in 3.2.

3.1.1 Small and medium-sized groups

Small and medium-sized groups are exempt from the requirement to prepare consolidated accounts. This exemption may only be claimed if the parent company's auditors provide the directors with a report stating that in their opinion the company is entitled to the exemption. The report must be attached to the parent company's accounts. Where advantage is taken of this exemption, certain disclosures are required in the parent company's accounts concerning its subsidiary undertakings (see 4.2.3 below). *S13(1) S248(3) &(4)*

Prior to the Act, small and medium-sized groups were required to prepare group accounts but were permitted to modify the group accounts delivered to the registrar. The Act no longer provides for the filing of modified group accounts so groups which have previously filed such accounts will have to file either unmodified group accounts or, if they satisfy the new criteria for exemption, no group accounts at all.

To qualify as small or medium-sized, a group must satisfy certain criteria based on the statutory accounts of companies within the group and on the number of employees of the group. The Act includes criteria for both small and medium-sized groups even though those relating to small groups appear to be redundant in that any group satisfying them will also satisfy the medium-sized group criteria. Their inclusion may well be intended to allow for the fact that future legislation could have an impact on small groups. For example, a proposal exists which would require member states to abolish the audit requirement for small companies. This particular proposal has so far been opposed by the Government. *S13(3) S249(3)*

In deciding whether the criteria are satisfied, all subsidiary undertakings must be taken into account even if the group is entitled to exclude some of them from consolidation.

Certain groups may not claim exemption even if they satisfy the criteria. These are groups which contain: *S13(3)* *S248(2)*

(a)   a public company or a body corporate other than a company (this would include foreign companies) whose constitution allows it to offer its shares or debentures to the public;

(b)   an authorised institution under the Banking Act 1987;

(c)   an insurance company to which Part II of the Insurance Companies Act 1982 applies; or

(d)   an authorised person under the Financial Services Act 1986.

There are two sets of financial limits for small or medium-sized groups, one based on aggregate figures from the accounts of group companies before making consolidation set-offs ('gross') and the other on aggregate figures after consolidation set-offs ('net'). If a group satisfies the criteria on either basis, it is exempt from preparing consolidated accounts. The bases can be mixed, i.e. one limit satisfied on a net basis, the other on a gross basis. The limits for the gross basis are approximately 20% higher than those for the net basis. *S13(1)& (3) S249(4)*

The use of the gross basis allows groups to claim exemption from preparing group accounts without having to perform a consolidation exercise to prove their entitlement. Some groups with a significant amount of intra-group trading are likely to have to use the net basis as they may not meet the gross limits. The net basis limits are the same as the existing limits which will continue to have effect for the purpose of individual companies filing modified accounts, except that the figure for the balance sheet total for a small group is £1 million compared to £975,000 for a small company.

Unlike the provisions for individual companies filing modified accounts, there is no requirement to adjust the turnover limit in respect of a financial year which is less than or more than 12 months in length.

The Act explains how the aggregate figures should be determined and defines 'balance sheet total' as the total of items A to D if Format 1 is used and the total under the heading 'Assets' if Format 2 is used. All the figures must be taken from statutory accounts. Management accounts are not allowed to be used for this purpose but are permitted, and in some cases required, as a basis for consolidated accounts (see 3.4 below). Some groups may find that, because of the different periods the accounts may cover, consolidated accounts prepared using management accounts give the impression that the group qualifies for the new exemption when this is not in fact the case. *S13(1) &(3) S249(4), S247(5) &(6)*

The rules for changing an existing status as a small, medium-sized or large group are the same as those for individual companies. This means that an existing status will only change in the second consecutive year in which a group fails to meet (or meets) two out of the three criteria. *S13(3) S249(1) &(2)*

In the first accounting reference period of the parent company, the group will *S13(3)*
qualify if it satisfies two out of the three criteria in that year.   *S249(1)*

The application of these rules can produce some rather unexpected results, some of
which may well not have been intended. For those readers who are interested in
pursuing this further, a series of examples is given in Appendix 3.

3.1.2   Intermediate holding companies

Wholly-owned subsidiaries of bodies corporate incorporated in Great Britain have   *S5(3)*
for many years been exempt from preparing group accounts. The Seventh   *S228(1)*
Directive replaces this by a new exemption which is available to intermediate
holding companies whose immediate parent undertaking is established in a member
state of the EC.

The new exemption is not confined to wholly-owned subsidiaries but is available   *S5(3)*
where the immediate parent holds more than 50% of the shares in a company.   *S228(1)*
Minority shareholders have the right to request the preparation of consolidated   *(b)&(3)*
accounts for a financial year by serving a notice on the company within 6 months
of the end of the previous financial year. The minority in question must hold more
than half of the shares in the company not held by the immediate parent or more
than 5% of the total shares of the company. The exemption does not apply to
companies having shares or debentures listed on a stock exchange in a member
state and is subject to the following conditions:

(a)   the company must be included in audited consolidated accounts of a parent   *S5(3)*
         undertaking established under the law of a member state and complying   *S228(2)*
         with the Seventh Directive. The accounts must be drawn up to the same   *(a)&(b)*
         date as the company's accounts or an earlier date during the same financial
         year;

(b)   the following disclosures must be given in the accounts of the company: *S5(3)*
                                                                                     S228(2)
                                                                                     (c)&(d)
         (i)   the fact that the company is exempt from preparing group
                  accounts; and

         (ii)   the name of the parent undertaking which drew up the accounts
                  referred to in (a) above; and

                  •   its country of incorporation, if incorporated outside Great
                           Britain;

                  •   if incorporated in Great Britain, whether it is registered in
                           England and Wales or in Scotland; or

                  •   if it is unincorporated, the address of its principal place of
                           business; and

(c)   the accounts referred to in (a) above must be delivered by the company to   *S5(3)*
       the registrar together with (if they are not in English) a certified English   *S228(2)*
       translation.   *(e)&(f)*

This exemption can result in the same set of group accounts being filed by a number of different companies and an example will show that it has some rather surprising effects.

Example 2   Exemption for intermediate parents

The A group has the following structure:

```
                                    A
                                    |
                                    B
                                    |
                                    C
                                    |
                                    D
```

All the subsidiary undertakings of A are 100% owned. The effect of the exemption on several different sets of circumstances will be considered as shown by the columns in the following table:

Company		Incorporated in	
	(a)	(b)	(c)
A	Great Britain	Netherlands	Netherlands
B	United States of America	France	Great Britain
C	Great Britain	Great Britain	Great Britain
D	Great Britain	Great Britain	Great Britain

(a)   A and C must both prepare group accounts. In the case of C, this is because its immediate parent is not incorporated in a member state. Under the 1985 Act, C would be exempt as a wholly owned subsidiary of a British company. Fortunately, the above structure is unlikely to arise frequently in practice as A would not be in the same UK tax group as C and D.

It would make no difference to the above if B were incorporated in the Channel Islands or the Isle of Man as these are not member states. Northern Ireland is part of a member state so if B were incorporated there, only A would have to prepare group accounts (this will be the position once the provisions of the Act have been applied to Northern Ireland and an Order in Council is required to do this). The combined effect of previous Companies Acts and Northern Ireland Orders has been that A and B would both be required to prepare group accounts in these circumstances.

(b)   C is exempt from preparing group accounts. If B as well as A chose to prepare consolidated accounts complying with the Seventh Directive, then the effect of the wording of new section 228(2) is that C could choose to file an English translation of either A or B's group accounts. Under the present rules, C would be required to prepare group accounts.

(c)   B and C are exempt from preparing group accounts but both companies must file an English translation of A's group accounts. If the B (or C) group were small or medium-sized it could claim exemption on grounds of size without having to file A's accounts. This could reduce duplication of filing to an extent but it means obtaining a report that in the auditor's opinion the group is entitled to the exemption claimed. Often this will be less costly and time-consuming than translating documents into English. However, this would not be of any assistance if the A group contained a public company, a bank or an insurance or financial services company. There is also the drawback that the disclosure requirements are more onerous where the exemption is claimed on grounds of size rather than as an intermediate parent company (see 4.2.3 below).

Intermediate parent companies which are wholly owned by foreign companies are often reluctant to prepare consolidated accounts. SSAP 14 can be read as exempting wholly owned subsidiaries of foreign as well as British companies so that their group accounts need comply only with the Companies Act. Since the 1985 Act permitted group accounts in other than consolidated form (see 3 above), some such groups filed all the individual accounts of group companies belonging to the British sub-group together as an alternative form of group accounts. This will no longer be possible since the Act requires group accounts to be consolidated accounts. Other groups in this position filed no group accounts at all, arguing that the preparation of group accounts would cause expense or delay out of proportion to their value to the members. A similar exemption now exists, so doubtless there will be pressure to use it, especially from companies with non-EC parents, although the wording of the exemption is rather narrower than before, as will be seen in the discussion which follows on the circumstances in which subsidiaries may be excluded from consolidation (see 3.2.1 below).

It is a pity that it has not been found possible to implement a member state option which would have permitted subsidiaries of non-EC parents not to file group accounts provided they filed a world-wide consolidation giving equivalent information to Seventh Directive accounts. This particular option seems to be proving rather difficult for any member state to implement successfully, especially since a European Court decision that the Netherlands could not carry through a proposal to treat International Accounting Standards as equivalent to Seventh Directive accounts. Given that International Accounting Standards at present allow a wide range of options, this may seem unsurprising. However, a significant factor in the decision seems to have been that International Accounting Standards are set by a private rather than a public sector body and it is possible that this may apply to the standards of various other non-EC countries, including the USA.

3.2 Subsidiary undertakings excluded from consolidation

Subsidiary undertakings may be excluded from consolidation in certain circumstances; if such circumstances apply to all subsidiary undertakings, no group accounts are required. The law no longer permits subsidiaries to be excluded on the grounds that it would be harmful to the business to consolidate them. This exemption required the Secretary of State's approval and was seldom used. Neither does it permit exclusion on the grounds that it would be misleading to consolidate; in effect, the new rules spell out the circumstances in which it would be misleading. The new rules are discussed below and, where an equivalent rule exists, compared with SSAP 14 and the previous statutory rules. *S5(3) S229(5)*

It should be noted that the new rules relate to circumstances under which subsidiary undertakings may be excluded from consolidation rather than from any form of group accounts, in contrast to the previous statutory rules.

Paragraph 21(b) of SSAP 14 contains an exclusion on the grounds of lack of effective control which is not reflected in the Act. However, given the change in emphasis in the new definitions from majority equity ownership to majority voting control, this situation is now less likely to arise.

3.2.1 Disproportionate expense or undue delay

The previous rules allow subsidiaries to be excluded from group accounts if their inclusion would cause expense or delay out of proportion to the value to the members. There is a new similar provision but it no longer looks at the expense or delay in proportion to the value to the members; in fact, the word 'disproportionate' is used without any explanation of what it relates to. As already mentioned (see 3.1.2 above), intermediate holding companies with non-EC parents may consider taking advantage of this provision. *S5(3) S229 (3)(b) S229 (3)(b) CA85 (rep)*

It would seem that companies will no longer be able to justify using this exemption based solely on the wishes of their members. However, it is not at all clear which persons other than members would be considered to have a legitimate interest in the preparation of consolidated accounts nor is there any specific mechanism for such persons to challenge a company's decision not to prepare consolidated accounts. However, it is possible that the new rules on revision of defective accounts might be used to challenge such a decision (see Chapter 2 at 10.2). Nevertheless, companies which have taken advantage of the old exemption for a number of years without receiving complaints from any direction may well conclude that they are entitled to take advantage of the new exemption.

3.2.2 Interests held for resale

The Act permits a subsidiary undertaking to be excluded from consolidation if it is held solely with a view to resale and it has not previously been included in the consolidated accounts. This corresponds to the SSAP 14 exeption for *S5(3) S229 (3)(c)* subsidiaries where control is intended to be temporary. However, the new statutory exclusion cannot be used to justify exclusion of a subsidiary which the parent company has previously consolidated and decides to sell some time after its acquisition.

The previous statutory rules contained no similar exclusion. The exclusion from consolidation of subsidiaries held for resale had to be justified on the grounds that it would have been misleading to consolidate them. Paragraph 27 of SSAP 14 requires subsidiaries excluded on these grounds to be included as current assets in the consolidated balance sheet at the lower of cost and net realisable value. *S229(3) (c)CA85 (rep)*

3.2.3 *Dissimilar activities*

Previously, the Secretary of State's approval was required for excluding a subsidiary from group accounts on the grounds of dissimilar activities. In fact, this exemption was not used in practice because, in such circumstances, subsidiaries were excluded from consolidation rather than from any form of group accounts. Paragraph 21(a) of SSAP 14 permits this and was commonly applied where the group contained some companies preparing accounts under Schedule 4 and others under Schedule 9 (banks and insurance companies). It also tended to be used by retail groups to justify excluding their finance subsidiaries. *S5(3) S229(4) S229(3) (d)&(4) CA85 (rep)*

The new statutory provision makes it clear that dissimilar activities means more than just diverse activities such as the provision of goods as well as services, and manufacturing as well as retail or other commercial activities. It remains to be seen how this will be interpreted, but there must be some doubt as to whether retail groups may continue to exclude their finance subsidiaries from consolidation. The activities of such subsidiaries are closely linked to the mainstream operations of the group and it is therefore arguable that they ought to be consolidated.

Where a subsidiary is excluded from consolidation on these grounds, the Act requires it to be equity accounted. Paragraph 23 of SSAP 14 also requires this and in addition requires separate financial statements to be included giving the following information: *18Sch2 18Sch4A*

(a)   a note of the holding company's interest;

(b)   particulars of intra-group balances;

(c)   the value of transactions with the rest of the group; and

(d)   a reconciliation with the group's investment in the subsidiary in the consolidated accounts.

Where the new exclusion is used and the subsidiary undertakings excluded include either: *S11 S243*

(a)   a body corporate incorporated outside Great Britain which does not have an established place of business in Great Britain; or

(b)   an unincorporated undertaking

the latest accounts (or group accounts) of any such undertaking must be appended to the accounts delivered to the registrar. However, this does not require the preparation of accounts which would otherwise not be prepared. Neither does it require the publication of accounts which would not otherwise be required to be published but the reason for such accounts not being appended must be explained. For example, a partnership excluded on these grounds might prepare accounts for its own purposes; however these would not need to be appended provided the accounts delivered to the registrar contained a note to the effect that the partnership accounts were not appended as they were not required to be published. In the case of foreign companies, this means that, for example, the accounts of a Canadian company would have to be appended but not those of most US companies (since US companies, other than those with a SEC listing, are not required to publish their accounts).

In the case of banking and insurance groups, undertakings may not be excluded on these grounds if their activities are a direct extension of, or ancillary to, the banking or insurance business.

1 Part II
Sch7
1 Part II
Sch9

3.2.4   *Severe long-term restrictions*

This exclusion is new to the law and corresponds to paragraph 21(c) of SSAP 14 which is most commonly applied in the context of subsidiaries operating in countries which place restrictions on the movement of assets (such as exchange control restrictions limiting the subsidiary's ability to pay dividends). The treatment required by SSAP 14 in these circumstances is to 'freeze' the carrying value of the subsidiary under equity accounting at the time the restrictions came into force, and not to accrue for any trading results thereafter as long as the restrictions remain. However, a provision for permanent impairment in value of the investment may be needed.

S5(3)
S229
(3)(a)

Paragraph 26 of SSAP 14 requires the following disclosures to be made in respect of a subsidiary excluded on these grounds:

(a)   net assets;

(b)   profit or loss for the period covered by the group accounts; and

(c)   amounts included in the consolidated profit and loss account in respect of:

(i)   dividends received; and

(ii)   writing down of the investment.

The Act contains a condition that the rights which are restricted must be rights in the absence of which the company would not be the parent company. This may well make the exclusion more restrictive than at present (it is doubtful whether exchange control restrictions would be a sufficient reason for exclusion).

Therefore, groups presently applying the equivalent SSAP 14 exclusion should review the position to ensure that the Act still permits them to do so.

3.2.5   Materiality

The new version of the exclusion makes it clear that two or more subsidiary undertakings may only be excluded if their combined effect is 'not material', in contrast to the previous wording which allowed subsidiaries to be excluded if individually the amounts involved were 'insignificant'. This should not have any practical effect as it would be inconsistent with SSAP 14 to exclude from consolidation subsidiary undertakings which were individually insignificant but the combined effect of which was material.

S5(3)
S229(2)
S229
(3)(a)
CA85
(rep)

3.3   Approval of parent company balance sheet and profit and loss account

The Act clarifies the statutory approval requirements for a parent company's individual profit and loss account which has been incorporated into a consolidated profit and loss account. The old approval requirement which is being replaced is generally not interpreted as requiring the approval of the holding company's individual profit and loss account but there is a new approval requirement specifically referring to it. Under the Act, although the individual profit and loss account must be approved by the board of directors, it may be omitted from the company's annual accounts for filing and other purposes. The version presented to the board for approval should comply with one of the statutory profit and loss account formats but the Schedule 4 supplementary note disclosures need not be given. This seems to strike a reasonable balance, in that it requires the directors to see and approve the parent company's contribution to the consolidated profit and loss account on a line-by-line basis without going so far as to require detailed statutory disclosures which will never be published. The parent company's published accounts must contain the following disclosures which are equivalent to those required prior to the Act:

S5(4)
S230

(a)   the amount of the parent company's profit or loss for the financial year; and

(b)   the fact that the parent company is relying on the statutory exemption from publishing its own profit and loss account.

Where consolidated accounts are prepared, only the parent company balance sheet is required to be signed although the consolidated accounts must be approved by the directors. In this respect, the statutory approval requirement remains unchanged but no doubt it will remain common practice for consolidated as well as parent company balance sheets to be signed.

S7
S233

3.4 Non-coterminous year ends

Directors should ensure that the financial years of subsidiary undertakings coincide with that of the parent company, except where there are good reasons for using different periods. A similar requirement existed under the previous statutory accounting rules.

S3
S223(5)

Where a subsidiary's year end does not coincide with that of its holding company, the Companies Acts have for many years required group accounts to deal with the subsidiary's most recent financial year ending before that of the holding company. Interim accounts dealing with the period between the two year ends (or part of that period) could only be used with the approval of the Secretary of State. The Act makes the following changes:

2(2)Sch2
2(2)
Sch4A

(a)   interim accounts *must* be used if the financial year of the subsidiary undertaking ends more than three months before that of the parent company;

(b)   the interim accounts used must be made up to the parent company's year end; and

(c)   the Secretary of State's approval for the use of interim accounts will no longer be needed.

3.5 Basis and method of preparing group accounts

Prior to the Act, there were no detailed statutory provisions on the preparation of consolidated accounts. Schedule 4 to the 1985 Act confined itself to saying that consolidated accounts should be based on the accounts of the holding company and its consolidated subsidiaries with such adjustments as the directors of the holding company considered necessary. Also, as a general rule, Schedule 4 required consolidated accounts to comply with the accounting requirements of the 1985 Act as if they were the accounts of a company. This continues to be the case, but the Act requires group accounts to be in consolidated form and introduces a new Schedule to be inserted as Schedule 4A to the 1985 Act. This contains rules on the preparation of consolidated accounts as well as certain disclosure requirements. To a large extent, these rules codify existing practice although certain changes are made, most notably to the requirements for merger accounting. An amendment to Schedule 4 restricting the use to which a revaluation reserve may be put has an impact on the treatment of goodwill in consolidated accounts.

The Act also includes a provision relating to the accounting records of subsidiary undertakings not subject to Companies Act requirements. This requires the parent company to take reasonable steps to ensure that such accounting records provide the information required by the Act in relation to group accounts and disclosures in the accounts of the parent company.

2
221(4)

3.5.1   Conditions for merger accounting

Prior to the Act, there were no statutory restrictions on the use of merger accounting, although the Companies Acts had paved the way for its use by introducing relief from setting up a share premium account in certain circumstances. SSAP 23 therefore contains the only pre-existing restrictions on the use of merger accounting. The Act preserves the present position that merger accounting is available as an option provided certain conditions are satisfied. The DTI considered a number of other options, including a prohibition on merger accounting, but following consultation it was decided to adopt an approach which does not go far beyond the minimum required by the Seventh Directive. The conditions for merger accounting both under the Act and under SSAP 23 are summarised in the following table:

Table 3.1:   Comparison of merger accounting criteria in the Act and in SSAP 23

SSAP 23 paragraph 11	Schedule 2 paragraph 10
1. The group holds at least 90% of each class of equity shares of the subsidiary and shares carrying at least 90% of the votes.	1. The group holds at least 90% of the nominal value of the 'relevant shares' (see below) of the undertaking.
2. The subsidiary was acquired as a result of an offer to the holders of all its equity shares and all its voting shares not already held by the group.	2. The proportion referred to in 1. was obtained as a result of an arrangement involving the issue of equity shares of one or more group undertakings.
3. Immediately prior to the offer, the group holds less than 20% of each class of equity shares of the subsidiary and the shares it holds carry less than 20% of the votes.	3. No equivalent requirement.
4. At least 90% of the fair value of the total consideration given for the equity share capital is in the form of equity share capital; at least 90% of the fair value of the total consideration given for voting non-equity share capital is in the form of equity and/or voting non-equity share capital.	4. The fair value of any consideration given under the arrangement other than equity shares did not exceed 10% of the nominal value of the equity shares issued.

In addition, paragraph 10 of Schedule 2 requires that the adoption of the merger method of accounting accords with generally accepted accounting principles or practice.

'Relevant shares' are defined as being those carrying unrestricted rights to participate both in distributions and in surplus assets on a winding up. Such shares will necessarily be equity shares since 'equity share capital' is defined as 'issued share capital excluding any part of that capital which neither as respects

10(2)
Sch2
10(2)
Sch4A
S744
CA85

dividends nor as respects capital, carries any right to participate beyond a specified amount in a distribution'. This means that satisfaction of condition 1 above in relation to SSAP 23 will automatically ensure satisfaction of the corresponding statutory restriction.

It can be seen from the above that:

(a)   the Act effectively gives statutory backing to SSAP 23 by requiring that the use of merger accounting must accord with generally accepted accounting principles or practice; and

(b)   the SSAP 23 conditions are generally more restrictive than the Act except in relation to the fourth condition in the above table. This stricter condition included in the Act is required by the Seventh Directive. It will not affect transactions where the consideration is settled solely by the issue of equity shares but if even a small proportion of the fair value of the consideration is in a form other than the issue of equity shares, merger accounting may no longer be available.

It is expected that the new conditions will only be brought into effect for acquisitions occurring in accounting periods commencing on or after a particular date (probably January 1, 1990) so that groups will not be required to amend the treatment of acquisitions occurring prior to that date.

In future, companies which fail to satisfy the new statutory restriction discussed in (b) above with a particular proposed consideration may find that the condition is satisfied if reserves are capitalised. This effectively increases the nominal value element of the consideration, as is shown by the following example:

Example 3   *Effect of capitalisation of reserves on statutory restrictions on merger accounting*

A company is proposing to give the following consideration to acquire another company:

	Market Value £000	Nominal Value £000
£1 equity shares — market value £5 per share	500	100
Cash	20	20
	520	120

The cash consideration of £20,000 exceeds 10% of the nominal value of the equity shares (i.e. 10% x £100,000 = £10,000) so merger accounting could not be used under the new statutory rules.

Suppose that the company has the following capital and reserves structure:

	£000
£1 equity shares	2,000
Reserves	11,250
	13,250

If the company capitalises £2 million of its reserves, the nominal value of its equity shares will increase to £4 million but the total market value of the 4 million shares will (theoretically, at least) remain unchanged so that each share will have a market value of £2.50.

To satisfy the £500,000 equity consideration, the company will therefore issue 200,000 £1 equity shares with the following result:

	Market Value £000	Nominal Value £000
£1 equity shares — market value £2.50 per share	500	200
Cash	20	20
	520	220

The cash consideration of £20,000 is now equal to 10% of the nominal value of the equity shares (i.e. 10% x £200,000) so the statutory restriction on the value of non-equity consideration is satisfied.

If it chooses, the company can redenominate its shares so that the market value of the individual shares remains unchanged at £5. In this case, this would be done by redenominating the 4 million £1 shares as 2 million £2 shares.

SSAP 23 is currently under revision and it is possible that a future standard will further restrict the use of merger accounting.

3.5.2   Goodwill

A change has been made to Schedule 4 which will affect goodwill arising on the purchase of a business as well as on consolidation. The change relates to the purposes for which the revaluation reserve may be used and can be summarised as follows:

6Sch1 34(3), (3A) &(3B) Sch4

(a)   a requirement that the reserve should be reduced to the extent that it has been credited with amounts which are 'no longer necessary for the purpose of the accounting policies adopted by the company' has been modified to require it to be reduced 'to the extent that the amounts transferred to it are no longer necessary for the purposes of the valuation method used';

(b)   a prohibition on the reduction of the revaluation reserve except as permitted by paragraph 34; and

(c)   a clarification that capitalisation of amounts standing to the credit of the revaluation reserve is permissible.

The third of these is merely a clarification but the first two are intended to prevent the practice which has been adopted by some companies of writing off goodwill on consolidation against revaluation reserve. The second implements a provision in the Fourth Directive which had not previously been included in the Companies Acts, possibly because other uses of revaluation reserve were not anticipated when the Directive was implemented in 1981.

Apart from the above, the Act does not have an impact on the treatment of goodwill so the following different treatments will still presumably continue to appear in accounts:

(a)   amortisation to profit and loss account;

(b)   immediate write off against accumulated revenue reserve;

(c)   immediate write off against merger reserve (a reserve created when relief from setting up a share premium account is taken but acquisition rather than merger accounting is used);

(d)   immediate write off against capital reserves arising on consolidation;

(e)   the creation of a negative goodwill write off reserve; and

(f)   the cancellation of share premium account by applying to the court for a reduction of capital and the subsequent use of the reserve created on cancellation for writing off goodwill.

When, in 1988, the DTI announced its legislative proposals on the subjects of merger relief, merger accounting and goodwill, it was clear that reductions in the options available for writing off goodwill had been considered but eventually it was decided only to clarify that the revaluation reserve is not available for this purpose. Option (f) is, however, being kept under review and it could eventually be removed.

The Act therefore does nothing to alleviate the position of those companies in service industries where acquisitions often lead to large amounts of goodwill resulting in considerably reduced or even negative reserves if the goodwill is written off immediately. There has been a tendency amongst such companies to avoid the less attractive option under SSAP 22 of amortising goodwill to profit and loss account by identifying and recognising intangible assets other than goodwill, such as brand names. This practice is likely to continue unless prevented by a future accounting standard.

3.5.3 *Consistency of accounting policies*

The Act includes provisions which appear similar to the requirement of paragraph 16 of SSAP 14 that uniform group accounting policies should be used in preparing consolidated accounts. The Act is differently phrased from the standard in that:

3&4
Sch2
3&4
Sch4A

(a)   it envisages the possibility of 'accounting rules' different from those used in the parent company's individual accounts being used in group accounts. SSAP 14 anticipates that the parent company's accounting policies will determine the treatment to be used in the group accounts; and

(b)   it refers to 'accounting rules' for valuing 'assets and liabilities' which is not necessarily the same thing as accounting policies because the latter relate also to items of income and expenditure.

If anything, paragraph 16 of SSAP 14 is a stricter requirement than that contained in the Act so it seems unlikely that there will be any significant change in existing practice. The Act does permit inconsistent accounting policies to be used in limited circumstances but details of the inconsistency must be disclosed (see 4.1.5 below).

3.5.4 *Elimination of intra-group transactions*

The requirement to eliminate intra group transactions has never been incorporated into an accounting standard in the UK although it is referred to in the explanatory note to SSAP 14 (paragraph 3). The Act now makes this practice a statutory requirement. As an alternative to completely eliminating unrealised intra-group profits and losses, the Act permits eliminations to be based on the proportion of the group's interests in the shares of its subsidiary undertakings. The first alternative is perhaps more usual but the second is also acceptable. It effectively regards the minority's share of the profit as realised and therefore not requiring elimination. Those preferring the first alternative would argue that no part of the profit is realised until the asset is sold outside the group.

6Sch2
6Sch4A

3.5.5 *Acquisition and merger accounting methods*

The Act describes the acquisition and merger methods of accounting in terms which are equivalent to the corresponding requirements of SSAP 23. This means that the following are now statutory requirements:

9,11&12
Sch2
9,11&12
Sch4A

(a)   under the acquisition method:

(i)   a fair value exercise must be performed;

(ii)   results of the undertaking or group acquired may be brought into the consolidated accounts only from the date of acquisition; and

(iii) positive consolidation differences must be treated as goodwill and negative differences as 'negative consolidation differences'. No new statutory rules are introduced on the treatment of such differences, except as discussed in 3.5.2 above. This means that there are no statutory rules on the accounting treatment of negative goodwill and that positive goodwill must (as at present), if treated as an asset, be written off over its useful economic life. Existing practice is therefore likely to continue unless affected by a future accounting standard; and

21 Sch4
CA85

(b) under the merger method:

(i) the acquired undertaking's (or group's, if a group was acquired) assets and liabilities should only be adjusted to bring them into line with group accounting policies rather than bringing them in at fair values;

(ii) no adjustment should be made in respect of the results of the undertaking or group prior to its acquisition;

(iii) comparative figures should be adjusted as if the undertaking or group had been owned throughout the financial year of the parent company preceding that in which the acquisition took place; and

(iv) any consolidation difference between the nominal value of the shares in the undertaking held by the group and the aggregate of the 'appropriate amount' of the 'qualifying shares' issued as consideration and the fair value of any other consideration should be shown as an adjustment to the consolidated reserves. The formats have not been adapted to provide appropriate captions for this difference. 'Qualifying shares' means shares which qualify for relief from setting up a share premium account under either section 131 or section 132 of the 1985 Act. 'Appropriate amount ' means the nominal amount of the qualifying shares together with any minimum premium value under section 132.

Although the Act provides for acquisition costs to be included in the consolidation difference arising under acquisition accounting, it does not do so in relation to merger accounting. Prior to the Act, it was the usual practice to include these costs in the consolidation difference under both methods and this is likely to continue, if only because the costs are often immaterial in the context of the group accounts.

3.5.6 *Proportional consolidation of joint ventures*

Proportional consolidation is commonly used for oil company joint ventures and involves incorporating the investor's share of the assets, liabilities, income and expenditure in its accounts on a line by line basis. There is no accounting standard

19 Sch2
19 Sch4A

on this subject although SSAP 1 recognises that it may be appropriate in some cases for partnerships or non-corporate joint ventures. The Act permits proportional consolidation for certain joint ventures and the following points are worth noting:

(a)   the Act restricts proportional consolidation to unincorporated joint ventures. Incorporated joint ventures will therefore generally be equity accounted as associated undertakings. This subject was discussed during the House of Lords debate at the Report Stage of the Bill and the following reasons were given for not allowing proportional consolidation for corporate joint ventures:

   (i)   SSAP 1 requires equity accounting to be used in such cases and this is the usual practice;

   (ii)   there is no demand to change the present position; and

   (iii) a distinction ought to be drawn between corporate and non-corporate joint ventures. The latter equate to a direct interest in the underlying assets and liabilities whereas the former do not because the joint venture is a separate legal entity. (This ignores the fact that unincorporated joint ventures which may be proportionally consolidated include Scottish partnerships which are separate legal entities.)

   The argument that a separate legal entity is relevant in relation to group accounts is questionable. The whole purpose of consolidated accounts is to present the accounts of the companies comprising the group as one economic unit, thus ignoring the separate legal entities. However, groups with corporate joint ventures seem to prefer equity accounting to proportional consolidation. Certainly, the former will often generate a lower gearing than the latter. If, for any reason, a substantial demand for proportional consolidation for corporate joint ventures emerges, it is to be hoped that this question will be reconsidered;

(b)   the Act requires that the joint venture should be managed 'jointly with one or more undertakings not included in the consolidation' but otherwise places no restriction on the type of non-corporate joint venture which may be proportionally consolidated;

(c)   the Act permits proportional consolidation in group accounts but contains no provisions allowing such a treatment in individual company accounts. It could be inferred from this that such a treatment is not intended to be permitted. However, it is arguable that proportional consolidation ought to be adopted in individual accounts on the basis that there is in effect a direct interest in a proportion of the assets, liabilities, income and expenditure of the joint venture; and

(d)   the Act contains no detailed description of the proportional consolidation method, stating merely that 'the provisions of this Part relating to the preparation of consolidated accounts apply, with any necessary modifications, to proportional consolidation under this paragraph'. Now that the method is recognised in law, perhaps an accounting standard dealing with the subject will be developed.

Certain disclosures are required in relation to joint ventures which are proportionally consolidated (see 4.2.6 below).

3.5.7   Minority interests

No detailed rules are introduced concerning the calculation of minority interests but the new disclosure requirements make it clear that minority interests are amounts 'attributable to shares in subsidiary undertakings included in the consolidation held by or on behalf of persons other than the parent company and its subsidiary undertakings'. The statutory formats have been adapted to include minority interests (see 4.1.4 below).

17Sch2
17Sch4A

3.5.8   Associated undertakings

The Act requires equity accounting to be used for associated undertakings. The meaning of this term has already been discussed (see 2.5 above). The Act does not elaborate on what is meant by the equity method but presumably this is intended to be taken from SSAP 1, the relevant accounting standard. It does, however, make it clear that any goodwill element should be dealt with in accordance with paragraph 21 of Schedule 4. This would effectively require either immediate write off or amortisation of the goodwill element. Such a treatment is required by SSAP 22 but is not always found in practice. It would seem that groups which are materially affected will have to revise their accounting treatment.

22Sch2
22Sch4A

4   CONTENT OF ACCOUNTS

Many of the changes made to the required contents of accounts are minor consequences of the matters already discussed in this chapter. In effect, these substitute the new terminology for the old. This will affect the accounts of individual companies within a group as well as the group accounts. The effects of this on the formats for both individual and group accounts are shown in Appendix 2.

A number of new disclosure requirements are introduced and changes are made to existing requirements. Those affecting group accounts are discussed below. Certain changes are also made to the circumstances in which a group can avail itself of the banking and insurance company exemptions. These are discussed in more detail at 4.3.1 below.

4.1   New disclosures in group accounts

To a large extent, the new disclosure requirements discussed below originate from
the Seventh Directive. The disclosures relating to acquisitions and goodwill go
beyond the Seventh Directive requirements. Their inclusion in the Act reflects
criticism that disclosures relating to these matters in some published accounts are
not sufficiently informative.

The disclosures relating to acquisitions, disposals and goodwill (see 4.1.1, 4.1.2   16Sch2
and 4.1.3 below) are not required in relation to an undertaking incorporated or   *16Sch4A*
operating outside the UK if the directors of the parent company consider that
disclosure would be seriously prejudicial to the business of any group undertaking.
The Secretary of State must agree that the information need not be disclosed.

4.1.1   Acquisitions

The following details are required in relation to each acquisition taking place during   13Sch2
the financial year: *13Sch4A*

(a)   the name of the undertaking acquired or, if a group was acquired, of the
       parent undertaking of that group;

(b)   whether acquisition or merger accounting has been used; and

(c)   in relation to acquisitions significantly affecting the group accounts:

       (i)   the composition and fair value of the consideration given by the
               reporting group;

       (ii)   the profit or loss of the undertaking or group acquired for the
               period from the beginning of its financial year until the date of the
               acquisition and for its previous financial year;

       (iii)   where acquisition accounting has been used, a table must be given
               showing the book values immediately prior to acquisition and the
               fair values at the time of acquisition of each class of assets and
               liabilities of the undertaking or group acquired as well as the
               goodwill (positive or negative) arising. Any significant
               adjustments must be explained; and

       (iv)   where merger accounting has been used, any significant
               adjustments must be explained and adjustments to consolidated
               reserves must be disclosed, including the restatement of opening
               reserves.

To an extent, this reflects existing practice but it goes further in that (c) (iii) is a
new requirement. In fact, it corresponds closely with SSAP 22 (Revised) which
refers to 'major categories' of assets and liabilities and presumably this is indicative
of how 'classes' in this context will be interpreted. Both the Act and the revised
standard have developed in parallel and their motivation was to improve the present

standard of disclosure in relation to acquisitions. The fact that some companies had failed to disclose the true amount of goodwill arising on acquisitions was a particular cause of concern.

It should be noted that, where merger accounting has been used, (c)(ii) is additional to the SSAP 23 requirement to analyse consolidated earnings and extraordinary items between the period before and the period after the merger. In relation to acquisition accounting, (c)(ii) is additional to the SSAP 14 and 23 requirements that there should be sufficient information about the results of subsidiaries acquired to enable shareholders to appreciate the effect on consolidated results.

4.1.2   Goodwill

The Act requires the disclosure of the cumulative amount of goodwill written off *14Sch2* net of goodwill relating to subsidiaries disposed of. This may not be difficult for *14Sch4A* groups which amortise goodwill on consolidation but is bound to cause difficulties for some groups whose goodwill has been completely eliminated against reserves in the consolidated accounts. Some commentators have argued that companies ought to retain records of the goodwill acquired in relation to all subsidiaries still owned as such goodwill has never been reflected in the profit and loss account and should therefore be brought into account in computing the ultimate profit or loss when a subsidiary is disposed of. The requirement to disclose cumulative goodwill written off would appear to make the retention of such records a necessity and, in any event, they will be needed to comply with SSAP 22 (Revised).

There is no equivalent requirement in relation to the treatment of negative goodwill although it would be logical to apply the same principle to the extent that negative goodwill has not been reflected in the consolidated profit and loss account. The formats have not been adapted to insert appropriate captions for negative goodwill.

4.1.3   Disposals

If a subsidiary undertaking or group significantly affecting the group accounts has *15Sch2* been disposed of during the financial year, the following information must be *15Sch4A* given:

(a)   its name; and

(b)   the profit or loss for the period attributable to the undertaking or group disposed of.

4.1.4   Minority interests

The formats are adapted in the case of group accounts to insert captions for *17Sch2* 'minority interests' in both the balance sheet and profit and loss account (see *17Sch4A* Appendix 2 for the effect this will have on accounts). In the case of the balance sheet, there is a choice of position if Format 1 is used: 'Minority interests' may appear either immediately before or immediately after capital and reserves. This means that groups may, as at present, either deduct minority interests from net assets or include them in shareholders' funds.

4.1.5   Inconsistent accounting policies

3.5.3 refers to a general requirement that adjustments should normally be made in the consolidated accounts to bring the accounting policies of individual undertakings included in the consolidation into line with the group accounting policies.

If there are 'special reasons', it is permissible not to adjust but in such cases details 3&4Sch2
3&4
Sch4A of the inconsistency must be given, including its financial effect and the reason for not adjusting. If the accounting policies of the parent company differ from those of the group, details of the difference are required together with the reasons for using different policies. Disclosure of the financial effect is required if no adjustment is made in the consolidated accounts.

It is to be hoped that such disclosures will be extremely rare since uniform accounting policies for a group are required by paragraph 16 of SSAP 14 and it is a long-established convention that the accounting policies of the parent company determine the group accounting policies.

4.2   Related undertakings

Schedule 3 to the Act inserts a new Schedule 5 into the 1985 Act which recasts all the existing statutory disclosures relating to parent companies and to subsidiaries, related companies and other companies in which the reporting company has a significant interest. Disclosure requirements relating to directors' emoluments have been moved from Schedule 5 to Schedule 6 (see Chapter 2 at 2.1). A number of other changes are made; some of these are required by the Seventh Directive but others are made in an attempt to rationalise the existing requirements and bring them together because some of them presently appear in Schedule 4 while others appear in Schedule 5. The existing requirements are a frequent source of confusion and, despite the rationalisation, they remain complex. The more important features of the new Schedule are discussed below.

4.2.1   Companies not required to prepare group accounts

The Schedule is divided into two parts: Part I deals with disclosures to be given by companies not required to prepare group accounts and Part II with disclosures to be given by companies required to prepare group accounts. Part I applies even if a company chooses to prepare group accounts although not required to do so. This is unfortunate because some of the disclosures which will be required seem irrelevant in these circumstances, e.g. separate financial information about undertakings included in the group accounts. Other disclosures which seem appropriate in the circumstances, and therefore should preferably be given, are not actually required, e.g. details of joint ventures which are proportionally consolidated.

The reason why the company is not required to prepare group accounts must be given. A similar disclosure requirement existed prior to the Act but this will now extend to circumstances where the new exemption for intermediate holding companies applies (discussed in 3.1.2 above) as well as the exemption for small and medium-sized groups (discussed in 3.1.1 above). If the reason is that each subsidiary undertaking is excluded under one of the grounds discussed in 3.2 above, then the exclusion used for each subsidiary undertaking must be identified. *1(4)&(5) Sch3 1(4)&(5) Sch5*

4.2.2 Omission from accounts of disclosures concerning related undertakings

The disclosures required by Schedule 5 need not be given in the following circumstances:

(a)   if compliance with any of the provisions would, in the opinion of the directors, result in information of excessive length being given. In these circumstances, the information need only be given in respect of : *S6(1) S231(5) &(6)*

    (i)   the undertakings whose results or financial position, in the opinion of the directors, principally affected the accounts; and

    (ii)   subsidiary undertakings excluded from consolidation other than on materiality grounds.

    The accounts must make it clear that the information disclosed has been restricted in the manner described above and the next annual return of the reporting company must contain both the information disclosed and that omitted from the accounts.

    Schedule 5 requires certain disclosures when merger relief (i.e. relief from recognising a share premium, which applies where at least a 90% holding in a subsidiary is acquired and the consideration takes the form of shares) has been taken and these may never be excluded on the grounds described above; and

(b)   information may be excluded in relation to an undertaking if the following conditions are satisfied: *S6(1) S231(3)&(4)*

    (i)   it is established under the law of a country outside the UK or carries on business outside the UK;

    (ii)   in the opinion of the directors, disclosure would be seriously prejudicial to the undertaking in question or any member of the group; and

    (iii)   the Secretary of State agrees to the omission of the information.

The accounts must state the fact that the information has not been disclosed.

The above exclusion may not be applied to the requirement to disclose shares in and debentures of a company held by its subsidiary undertakings nor to the requirement for groups not required to prepare group accounts to disclose the aggregate amount of their total investment in subsidiary undertakings by the equity method of valuation.

4.2.3   *Disclosures relating to subsidiary undertakings*

If the reporting company or group has subsidiary undertakings, the disclosures relating to those undertakings remain much as before. Certain financial information must be given in the case of a parent company not required to prepare group accounts or in the case of subsidiary undertakings excluded from consolidated accounts. The details to be given are the same as those previously required for companies not preparing group accounts (but see 4.2.1 above concerning the effect that this will have on companies which voluntarily prepare group accounts). These disclosures, and their interrelationship with the disclosures required by SSAP 14 in relation to subsidiaries excluded from consolidation (see 3.2.3 and 3.2.4 above), frequently gave rise to confusion. The removal of the distinction between exclusion from consolidation and exclusion from group accounts (see 3.2 above) should help to alleviate this, as should the proposed revision of SSAP 14.

There is a new requirement to disclose, in relation to each subsidiary undertaking, the reason why it is a subsidiary undertaking of its immediate parent undertaking. This requirement will usually not apply as disclosure need not be made where the reason is that a majority of voting rights are held and the proportion of total shares held by the immediate parent undertaking is the same as the proportion of voting rights held. 15(5)
Sch3
15(5)
Sch5

It should also be emphasised that all the disclosures relating to subsidiary undertakings must be given by small and medium-sized groups as well as by groups not preparing group accounts because each subsidiary undertaking is excluded under one of the provisions discussed in 3.2 above. This contrasts with groups exempt from preparing group accounts because the parent company is an intermediate holding company. Such groups are not required to give financial information relating to subsidiary undertakings but must give the other disclosures required by the new Schedule 5. This can be seen from the following table which summarises all the requirements of the new Schedule 5 relating to subsidiary undertakings.

Table 3.2: Statutory disclosure requirements relating to subsidiary undertakings

Disclosures required in respect of each subsidiary undertaking:

1.   Name.
2.   (a)   if incorporated outside Great Britain, country of incorporation;

      (b)   if incorporated in Great Britain, country of registration;

      (c)   if unincorporated, address of principal place of business.

3.   For each class of shares held:

      (a)   identity of the class;

      (b)   proportion of nominal value held.

4.   In 3 above, distinguish direct and indirect holdings.

Additional disclosures which may be required:

5.   For each subsidiary undertaking excluded from consolidation, name and reason for exclusion. See also 7 and 10.

6.   For each subsidiary undertaking, condition in new section 258(2) or (4) by virtue of which it is a subsidiary undertaking. This does not apply:

      (a)   if a majority of the voting rights is held and the immediate parent undertaking holds the same proportion of shares in the undertaking as it holds voting rights;

      (b)   to parent companies not required to prepare group accounts.

7.   Aggregate capital and reserves at the end of the financial year of each subsidiary undertaking ending with or last before that of the reporting company and profit or loss for that year. This does not apply:

      (a)   in relation to consolidated subsidiary undertakings;

      (b)   in relation to subsidiary undertakings included in consolidated accounts under the equity method of valuation;

      (c)   if the reporting company is exempt as an intermediate parent company from preparing group accounts;

      (d)   if it is not material;

      (e)   in relation to undertakings in which the reporting company holds less than 50% of the shares and which are not required to deliver a balance sheet to the registrar and do not otherwise publish their balance sheet.

8.   Aggregate total investment of the reporting company in subsidiary undertakings under the equity method. If this information is not available, the accounts should state this. This does not apply if the reporting company is:

      (a)   required to prepare group accounts; or

      (b)   exempt as an intermediate holding company from preparing group accounts. In this case, the directors must state their opinion that the aggregate value of the reporting company's investment is not less than the total amount at which it is included in the company's balance sheet.

9.   For each subsidiary undertaking whose financial year did not end with that of the company:

      (a)   reasons why the directors of the reporting company consider that the year ends should be different;

      (b)   date of last year end before that of the reporting company. Alternatively, where there are a number of subsidiary undertakings, the earliest and latest such dates may be given.

10.   Details of material qualifications in the audit reports of subsidiary undertakings. If this information is not available, the accounts should state this. For companies required to prepare group accounts, this is only required in relation to subsidiary undertakings excluded from consolidation.

11.   Number, description and amount of shares in and debentures of the company held beneficially by subsidiary undertakings (generally prohibited but see 2.4(a)).

12.   If arrangements attracting merger relief have been made during the financial year (i.e. relief from recognising a share premium, which applies where at least a 90% holding in a subsidiary is acquired and the consideration takes the form of shares):

       (a)   name of the other company;
       (b)   number, nominal value and class of shares allotted;
       (c)   number, nominal value and class of shares acquired;
       (d)   particulars of accounting treatment adopted;
       (e)   if the company is required to prepare group accounts, details of the extent to which and manner in which the consolidated profit or loss is affected by any profit or loss of the other company (or any of its subsidiary undertakings) which arose before the arrangement.

13.   If arrangements attracting merger relief were made during the financial year or either of the two preceding financial years, net profit or loss realised on disposal of shares in or fixed assets of the other company (or any of its subsidiary undertakings) together with an explanation of the relevant transactions.

4.2.4   *Disclosures relating to parent undertakings*

Certain new requirements are added to the present requirement to disclose the identity of the ultimate parent company and its place of incorporation. These relate to the parent undertaking of:

11,12,30 &31Sch3 11,12,30 &31Sch5

(a)   the largest group of undertakings for which group accounts are drawn up and of which the reporting company (or parent company of the reporting group) is a member; and

(b)   the smallest such group of undertakings.

In relation to each such parent undertaking, the following details must be given:

(a)   its name;

(b)   (i)   if incorporated outside Great Britain, its country of incorporation;

       (ii)   if incorporated in Great Britain, whether registered in England and Wales or in Scotland; and

       (iii) if unincorporated, the address of its principal place of business; and

(c)   if copies of its group accounts are available to the public, the address from which they may be obtained.

4.2.5   *Disclosures relating to associated undertakings*

Certain disclosures are required in relation to associated undertakings. These are the first four items in Table 3.2 above and are similar to the previous disclosure requirements for significant investments except that:

22Sch3 22Sch5

(a)   the previous requirements related only to investments directly held by the parent company of the reporting group rather than the group as a whole (the holding of the entire group is relevant by virtue of the definition of 'associated undertaking' which was discussed in 2.5 above); and

(b)   the proportion of each class of shares held must be given both for the parent company of the reporting group and the group as a whole.

The disclosures are required even in respect of associated undertakings which have not been equity accounted on materiality grounds, subject to the exemptions discussed in 4.2.2 above. This is intended to ensure that the information will be given in the annual return.

4.2.6   *Disclosures relating to joint ventures*

In relation to a joint venture which is proportionally consolidated (see 3.5.6 above), the following disclosures must be given: *21Sch3 21Sch5*

(a)   its name;

(b)   its principal place of business;

(c)   the factors on which joint management is based;

(d)   the proportion of the capital of the joint venture held by the group; and

(e)   where the financial year end of the joint venture did not coincide with that of the parent company of the reporting group, the date of its last year end (ending before the financial year end of the parent company).

4.2.7   *Disclosures relating to significant investments*

The main change in these requirements is that, for companies required to prepare group accounts, the disclosures must be given both for investments of the parent company of the reporting group and investments of the group as a whole. Previously, the disclosures only applied to investments of the parent company.   *23&26 Sch3 23&26 Sch5*

Subsidiary undertakings, joint ventures and associated undertakings are excluded from these requirements as there are specific disclosure requirements in respect of them (see 4.2.3, 4.2.5 and 4.2.6 above).

A holding is 'significant' for the purposes of these disclosures if either: *7,8,23,24,26 &27Sch3& 1PartIIISch*

(a)   it amounts to 10% or more of the nominal value of any class of shares in the undertaking (shares which are non-equity are disregarded in relation to banking companies or groups); or   *7 7,8,23,24,26 &27Sch5&1 PartIII Sch9*

(b)   the book value of the holding exceeds 10% of the company's (or group's) assets as stated in its accounts.

The disclosures to be given are the first three items in Table 3.2.

Companies must also make the disclosures under the seventh item in Table 3.2 in *9,25&* *28Sch3&* *1PartIII* relation to holdings which amount to 20% or more of the nominal value of the shares in the investee (again, shares which are non-equity are disregarded in relation *Sch7* to banking companies or groups). This information need not be given in the *9,25,&* *28Sch5&* *1PartIII* circumstances described in 7 (c), (d) and (e) in Table 3.2 ; neither is it required by a company not required to prepare group accounts if the aggregate investment is *Sch9* shown under the equity method.

4.3   Banking and insurance groups

The existing requirements relating to 'special category' companies and groups are replaced. These changes as they affect individual accounts are discussed in Chapter 2 at 5.4. The most important changes affecting group accounts are discussed below.

4.3.1   *Exemptions for group accounts of banking and insurance groups*

Until now, any group containing a bank or insurance company has been able to *S18(1)* *S255A* *(3)&(4)* prepare special category group accounts. Under the Act, the corresponding exemptions are only available to groups where:

(a)   the parent company is a banking or insurance company; or

(b)   banking or insurance is the predominant activity of the group. Where banking is the predominant activity, the group must contain an undertaking which is an authorised institution under the Banking Act 1987. 'Predominant' in this context is left open to interpretation.

The new Schedule 4A to the 1985 Act (see 3.5 above) applies to banking and *2PartII* *Sch7* *2PartII* *Sch9* insurance groups. This means that the matters discussed in 3.5 and 4.1 above are all relevant in relation to such groups. The general requirement that group accounts should comply with Schedule 4 as if they were the accounts of a company is modified to refer to Schedule 9, which contains the special provisions applying to the individual accounts of banks and insurance companies.

The new Schedule 5 to the 1985 Act also applies to such groups so the matters discussed in 4.2 above are relevant.

It remains possible for a parent company of a banking or insurance group not to be eligible for treatment as a banking or insurance company. This would mean that the company's own balance sheet and the directors' report would comply with the normal requirements while the consolidated profit and loss account and balance sheet would be prepared in accordance with Schedule 9 to the 1985 Act.

4.3.2 *Goodwill*

Under the 1985 Act, accounts prepared under Schedule 9 could combine goodwill, patents and trademarks as a single item. The Act requires that goodwill in the consolidated accounts of a banking or insurance group will have to be dealt with on the basis laid down in Schedule 4, i.e. it will have to be written off over its useful life if carried as a fixed asset. For reasons which are not apparent, this provision does not also apply to the individual accounts of a banking or insurance company.

3(1) PartII Sch7 3(1)Part IISch9

4.3.3 *Shares held as a result of a financial assistance operation*

New disclosure requirements are introduced where a banking group has a subsidiary undertaking which is a credit institution whose shares it holds as a result of a 'financial assistance operation with a view to its reorganisation or rescue'. The requirements, which apply only to subsidiary undertakings excluded from consolidation because the interest is held with a view to subsequent resale (see 3.2.2), are as follows:

6PartII Sch7 6Part II Sch9

(a)   the nature and terms of the operation must be disclosed;

(b)   a copy of the undertaking's accounts, including group accounts where relevant, must be appended to the accounts delivered to the registrar, together with a certified English translation, where relevant; and

(c)   the fact that such accounts are appended must be referred to in a note to the accounts to which they are appended.

This does not require the preparation of accounts which would not otherwise be prepared. Neither does it require the publication of accounts which would not otherwise be required to be published but the reason for such accounts not being appended must be explained.

Chapter 4

Company administration

1 SUMMARY

This Chapter deals with a variety of new provisions which relate primarily to company administration. The major changes are as follows:

(a)   the 'elective regime' for private companies: private companies may elect to carry out business by unanimous written resolution rather than by way of resolution passed at a general meeting; they may also elect to dispense with, or modify, certain company law requirements;

(b)   registration of company charges: the process of registration is improved and simplified, and there is a new regime for the registration of charges secured on the property of a registered oversea company;

(c)   annual returns: there is a modification of the basic duty to deliver annual returns and a simplification of the existing requirements as to their content; and

(d)   *ultra vires*: the Act further restricts the extent to which the doctrine will apply.

There are also provisions which, *inter alia,* abolish the doctrine of deemed notice and the requirement that every company must have a company seal; reduce both the threshold for a notifiable interest and the period for notification in relation to the disclosure of interests in shares; increase the monetary limits relating to directors' transactions; and widen the circumstances in which a company may give financial assistance in order to purchase its own shares for the purposes of an employees' share scheme.

2 ELECTIVE REGIME FOR PRIVATE COMPANIES

The Act has introduced certain new provisions which amend the 1985 Act. These are designed to simplify the procedures under which private companies operate. Although essentially deregulatory, the Government has tried to ensure certain safeguards exist to prevent abuse. These reforms, which originate from the proposals of the Institute of Directors' working group on company law reform, are based upon two main changes, namely that :

(a)   a private company can substitute the unanimous written agreement of its shareholders for resolutions of shareholders passed at a general meeting (i.e. written resolutions); and

(b)   a private company can opt out by unanimous resolution — either written or passed at a meeting — of certain company law requirements (the so-called 'elective regime') including the holding of annual general meetings and the laying of accounts and reports before a general meeting.

Although the original proposals were aimed at owner-managed companies, the Government took the view that, so long as members' interests were protected, the option to enter the elective regime should be extended to all private companies. The decision to introduce these reforms reflects the Government's acknowledgement that many private companies have been forced to comply with certain statutory requirements which to them are little more than unnecessary formalities. Moreover, the fact that unanimity of members is required by the new provisions effectively operates as a safeguard, in that each member has the ability to veto the proposed election. Only an ordinary resolution is needed to revoke an election.

2.1   Written resolutions

Anything that may be done by resolution of the company in general meeting, or by resolution of a meeting of any class of members of the company, may instead be effected by a unanimous written resolution. Written resolutions must be signed by, or on behalf of, all the members of the company, who at the date of the resolution would have been entitled to attend and vote at general meetings (or, in the case of a class of members, at meetings of the class in question). Accordingly, a meeting will not be necessary, nor any previous notice of the resolution. *S113(2) S381A(1)*

The document which is sent to a member and which contains the proposed resolution must state accurately the full terms of that resolution. All members of the company, or of a relevant class, as the case may be, must agree and sign the resolution. There is, however, no requirement that all the signatures should appear on a single document. *S113(2) S381A(2)*

A resolution passed in this way shall take effect as if it were passed at a general meeting. The date of the resolution (i.e. the date on which, for the purposes of the Act, it was passed), is the date when the last member to sign it, or a person acting on his behalf, does so. However, in circumstances where the company's auditors are entitled to serve a notice on the company requiring a meeting to be held, the date of the resolution is the date on which the resolution takes effect, as described in 2.1.1 below. *S113(2) S381A (3)-(5)*

The written resolution procedure may be used irrespective of the nature of the resolution that would otherwise be required, e.g. whether it is special or *S113(2) S381A(6)* ordinary, requires special notice or is one of the elective resolutions described in 2.2 below.

The introduction of the written resolution procedure merely provides private companies with an option to take advantage of simplified procedures. The ability of a private company to take this option cannot be restricted by any existing or future provision in the company's memorandum or articles.

2.1.1 Rights of auditors in relation to written resolutions

A copy of any proposed written resolution must be sent to the company's auditors. *S113(2)*
Under the 1985 Act, auditors have a right to receive notices and other *S381B(1)*
communications relating to general meetings and a right to attend and be heard, insofar as the business of the meeting concerns them as auditors. This right is retained by the Act. However, if the written resolution procedure is used, and the general meeting is, therefore, dispensed with, special provisions are necessary to preserve that right.

A company's auditors have been given power, where a written resolution which *S113(2)*
concerns them is proposed, to requisition, attend and be heard at any general *S381B*
meeting. The Act provides that a written resolution will not have effect unless the *(2)-(4)*
company's auditors notify the company that, in their opinion, either it does not concern them as auditors, or it does so concern them, but that it need not be considered by the company in general meeting (or by a meeting of a relevant class of company members). However, the auditors have only seven days in which to raise their concerns, otherwise the resolution will be effective. If the auditors receive a copy of a resolution after all the members have agreed to it, it will not have effect until the company receives the necessary notification or, as the case may be, the seven day period expires.

2.1.2 Recording of written resolutions

Where a written resolution is agreed to, the company will be required to record it in *S113(2)*
a book in the same way as the minutes of proceedings of a general meeting of the *S382A(1)*
company. The book should also contain a record of the signatures.

2.1.3 Written resolutions: exceptions and special procedures

The written resolution procedure cannot be used to remove either a director or an *S114(1)*
auditor before his period of office expires. *1Sch15A*

The Act contains a number of specific procedural adaptations relating to: *S114(1)*
3-8Sch
15A

(a)   the disapplication of pre-emption rights;

(b)   financial assistance for the purchase of a company's own shares;

(c)   the authority for the off-market purchase of, or a contingent purchase contract for, a company's own shares;

(d)   the approval for a payment out of capital in connection with the purchase or redemption by a company of its own shares;

(e)   the approval of a director's service contract; and

(f)   the funding of a director's expenditure in performing his duties.

In each of these cases, certain matters must be disclosed to the members before, or at the time that, the resolution is sent to them for signature. This ensures that documents which would otherwise have to be circulated with the notice of the meeting, or be present at the meeting, are made available to the members signing the resolution. In the case of (c) and (d), the resolution will be effective without the signatures of members whose shares are being bought.

It should be noted that a company will be prevented from using the written resolution procedure if it re-registers as a public company.

2.2   Election by a private company to dispense with certain requirements

2.2.1   *Elective resolutions*

A new procedure has been introduced which enables private companies to elect to dispense with, or modify, certain internal procedural requirements, in five main areas. Furthermore, a power has been granted to the Secretary of State to extend, by regulation, the elective procedures to other provisions of the 1985 Act. An integral part of this process is the requirement that a company must pass a new type of resolution, an 'elective resolution', to permit the necessary dispensation or modification.

S117

If the resolution is to be passed by the company in general meeting, at least 21 days' notice of the meeting must be given in writing. Such notice must state that an elective resolution is to be proposed, and give its terms. At the meeting, the resolution must be agreed to by all the members entitled to attend and vote at the meeting, either in person or by proxy. An elective resolution will be ineffective unless all of these requirements are met. Alternatively, the new written resolution procedure may also be used.

S116(2)
S379A(2)

The company can revoke an elective resolution at any time by passing an ordinary resolution. The passing, or revocation, of such resolutions must be effected in accordance with the new provisions of the Act, and any contrary provision in the company's articles will not take precedence. Not surprisingly, an elective resolution will cease to have effect if the company is re-registered as a public company.

S116(2)
S379A
(3)-(5)

Elective resolutions, and resolutions revoking them, are to be added to the list of resolutions which must be delivered to the registrar.

S116(3)
S380(4)
(bb)

2.2.2   *Elections permitted by the Act*

The provisions of the 1985 Act to which the elective procedures may be applied are as follows:

(a) Duration of authority for certain allotments

The 1985 Act restricts the duration of an authority for the directors to allot shares without the company's approval to a maximum period of five years. This period may be extended by elective resolution to a later specified date or even made indefinite. *S115(1) S80A (1)&(2)*

An authority granted for either an indefinite or a fixed period may be revoked or varied by a resolution of the company in general meeting or by written resolution. This applies equally to an authority that is contained in the company's articles. *S115(1) S80A(3)*

(b) Laying of accounts and reports before general meeting

The Act has enabled companies to elect to dispense with the requirement to lay accounts and reports before the company in general meeting. This provision (which is discussed in Chapter 2 at 5.1), together with the ability of a private company to dispense with the holding of annual general meetings (as outlined in (c) below), are the most significant reforms in this new deregulatory package.

(c) Annual general meetings

A private company may elect to dispense with the holding of annual general meetings (AGMs). This represents a major deregulatory reform, recognising that for companies whose directors are also the sole shareholders, the holding of such meetings is often an unnecessary formality. *S115(2) S366A(1)*

An election has effect in the year in which it is made and for subsequent years. However, any member may serve notice on the company, requiring the holding of an AGM in a particular year. Such a notice must be served at least three months before the end of the year to which it relates. *S115(2) S366A (2)&(3)*

If the election ceases to have effect (either because it is revoked or because the company re-registers as a public company — see 2.2.1 above), an AGM need not be held in the year the election ceases if less than three months of the year remain (unless a notice has previously been served requiring an AGM in that year). *S115(2) S366A(5)*

(d) Authorisation of short notice of a meeting

Under the 1985 Act, the consent of members holding 95 per cent. of the shares is needed in order to permit a company to hold a meeting at short notice. Private companies may now elect to reduce this figure, but not to less than 90 per cent. *S115(3) SS369(4) &378(3)*

(e) Annual appointment of auditors

A private company may elect to dispense with the obligation to appoint auditors annually (see Chapter 5 at 4.1.1). Where such an election has been made, the company's auditors shall be deemed to be re-appointed for each succeeding financial year on the expiry of the time for appointing auditors for that year. *S119 S386(1) &(2)*

3   REGISTRATION OF COMPANY CHARGES

In 1985, the Government commissioned Professor A. L. Diamond to consider, *inter alia*, the need to reform the law in relation to the registration of charges created by companies. In essence, the conclusions contained in his *Review of Security Interests in Property* reflected the need to have an efficient and up-to-date register of charges that fulfils its purposes without unnecessarily hindering legitimate business activities. To a large degree, these conclusions have been accepted by the Government and incorporated into the Act.

The provisions have been enacted essentially to secure three objectives. The main aim is to improve, simplify and speed up the registration system by reducing the amount of documentation that must be submitted to Companies House, and to make it easier to update information already on the register.

The second objective is to reduce the cost and effort of dealing with charges at Companies House.

Thirdly, the Act has set up a new regime for the registration of charges secured on the property of a registered oversea company. A number of case decisions have highlighted certain deficiencies in this area and it is hoped that these problems will be remedied by the new regime.

An important feature of Part IV of the Act is that, while under the 1985 Act there were provisions applicable to England and Wales, and separate provisions for Scotland, there is now, subject to certain exceptions, one set of provisions applicable to charges created by companies registered in either jurisdiction. As a result, the Act refers to charges registrable in Great Britain.

The new provisions and their likely effect are discussed below.

3.1   Charges requiring registration

A charge is defined as 'any form of security interest (fixed or floating) over property, other than an interest arising by operation of law'. 'Property' in this context includes future property.   S93 S395(2)

The Act has redefined the list of charges requiring registration in England and Wales as well as Scotland and extended, in particular, the registration requirements in relation to intellectual property rights. Charges on service marks, registered designs and design rights must now be registered. The requirement to register charges over moveable property by reference to the law on bills of sale, and the separate requirement to register charges over ships, aircraft or shares in ships, have been replaced by an all embracing requirement to register charges over any tangible (corporeal in Scotland) moveable property of a company other than money.   S93 S396(1) &(2)

In addition, the Secretary of State may, by regulation, add to or remove from the list, any description of charge.   S93 S396(4)

3.2   Registration of charges

The date of creation of a charge is of significant commercial importance to parties dealing with a company. Put simply, a secured party will want to be sure that the charge has priority over other creditors of the company. In the majority of cases, a charge is created when the instrument of charge is executed by the company and, in any other case, when an enforceable agreement is entered into by the company conferring a security interest intended to take effect immediately or upon the company acquiring an interest in property subject to the charge. However, there may be circumstances where it is unclear when the charge was in fact created. For example, in the case of a charge created in the UK which comprises property situated outside the UK, and which at that time requires further steps to be taken in order to make it valid under the law of the other country, the date of creation is the date on which it is executed, or granted if it is not formally executed, in the UK. It is not the date on which it becomes valid in the other country.

S103
S414(2)
&(4)

In Scotland, references to the date of creation of a charge are to:

S103
S414(3)

(a)   in the case of a floating charge, the date on which the instrument creating the floating charge is executed by the company; and

(b)   in any other case, the date on which the right of the person entitled to the benefit of the charge is constituted as a real right.

In an effort both to simplify and improve the process of registration, the Act has introduced several changes to the present system. It is worth noting that the Act deals with all charges created over physical moveable property but apparently leaves gaps in its coverage of non-physical property. For example, it appears that fixed charges on shares in a company will still be valid despite non-registration.

3.2.1   *Registrar to send copies of particulars and date of filing*

A company is still required to deliver to the registrar the particulars of any charge it creates and there will be a prescribed form in which this is to be done. It must do so within 21 days of the creation of the charge or, as the case may be, the date that it acquired property subject to the charge. The registrar must file the particulars in the register, noting the date that he received them. He must then send to both the company and the chargee, a copy of the particulars filed and their date of receipt. The note evidencing the date of receipt will be of particular importance to the chargee who will have proof that the particulars have been received for registration.

S95
S398(1),
(4)&(5)

The particulars may be delivered to the registrar by another person interested in the charge, who may recover from the company the cost of registration. In practice, charges are often registered by the chargee, who is most at risk if they are not registered. If a charge is registered by someone who is interested in it, but is neither the company nor the chargee, the registrar must send the details to that person also.

S95
S398(1),
(2)&(5)

3.2.2　Delivery of the instrument is not required

There is no longer a requirement to deliver to the registrar the instrument of charge or, in the case of Scotland, a certified copy thereof. As a result, the registrar will be unable to compare the form that is to be filed with the instrument of charge itself. This results in major changes to the effect of certificates issued by the registrar which, under the 1985 Act, were conclusive evidence that the provisions of the Act had been complied with. Without delivery of the instrument this can no longer be the case (see 3.2.3 below).

Nevertheless, a company must keep a register of its charges (whether registrable at Companies House or not) and copies of the instruments of charges available for inspection free of charge by any creditor or member of the company, or by other persons on payment of a fee. This will, therefore, enable the accuracy to be checked (see 3.3 below). *S101 SS411& 412*

3.2.3　Certificate of registration not issued unless requested

The obligation of the registrar to issue certificates in respect of all charges registered has not been retained by the Act. Nevertheless, any person may require the registrar to issue a certificate. It will state the date on which any specified particulars of, or other information relating to, a charge were delivered to the registrar and must be signed by the registrar or authenticated by his official seal. *S94 S397 (3)&(4)*

A certificate will constitute conclusive evidence that the specified particulars or other information were delivered to the registrar no later than the date stated in the certificate. Furthermore, it is presumed, unless the contrary is proved, that they were not delivered to the registrar earlier than that date. *S94 S397(5)*

3.2.4　Notice of matters disclosed on the register

The Act has abolished the doctrine of deemed notice (see also 6.3 below) subject to certain exceptions, one of which relates to a person taking a charge over a company's property. Such a person is deemed to have notice of any matter requiring registration which is disclosed on the register at the time the charge is created. However, in any other case, a person shall not be taken to have notice of any matter merely because it is disclosed on the register or, because he failed to search the register in the course of making such inquiries as he ought reasonably to have made. *S103 S416(1)& (2)*

It should be noted that these new provisions are expressed to have effect subject to any other statutory provision as to whether a person is to be taken to have notice of any matter disclosed on the register. *S103 S416(3)*

3.2.5　Errors, omissions and late filing

(a)　Registration without a court application

A significant change introduced by the Act is that there is no longer a requirement to obtain court approval either to register a charge out of time, or to correct certain inaccuracies in the registered particulars.

The Act provides that further particulars of a charge, supplementing or varying the registered particulars, may be delivered to the registrar for registration at any time. *S96 S401(1)*

Further particulars must be in prescribed form and signed by or on behalf of both the company and the chargee. However, if either of them refuses (or if the chargee is unavailable to sign), the court may, on the application of the company or the chargee, as the case may be, order that the further particulars be delivered without the signature. The registrar will file the further particulars in the register and make a note of the date of delivery to him. A copy of the particulars delivered and the note evidencing the date of delivery will be sent to the company, the chargee and any other person interested in the charge if that person had delivered the particulars to the registrar. A similar procedure exists where either the company or the chargee fails to sign a memorandum of a charge ceasing to affect the company's property (see 3.2.6 below). *S96 S401 (2)-(4) S103 S417(1)*

Where there is a failure to register the particulars of a charge within 21 days from its creation, or as the case may be, the date on which the acquisition of property subject to a charge was completed, the Act does not prohibit late delivery. However, while late delivery is possible, the security gained by possessing a charge will only take effect in relation to events occurring after the date of registration. This removes the requirement under the 1985 Act to apply to the court for permission to register the particulars out of time. Nevertheless, the company and its officers may still be liable to a fine for the failure to register in time. *S95 SS398(3) & 400*

(b) Effect of late delivery of, and errors and omissions in, particulars filed

The Act modifies the 1985 Act provision which makes a charge void against an administrator, liquidator or creditor of the company if the prescribed particulars are not delivered within the 21 day period. In particular, it clarifies that such a charge will also be void as against purchasers of an interest in, or a right over, property subject to the charge. However, the protection afforded to such parties is confined, in the case of an unregistered charge, to the period before the charge is belatedly registered. Accordingly, the charge, once registered, will be valid as against persons subsequently acquiring an interest in, or a right over, property, and subject to certain conditions in respect of insolvency, as against an administrator or liquidator. *S95 S399*

Where a charge is registered late and insolvency proceedings are commenced against the company before the end of the relevant period (defined below) beginning with the date of delivery of the particulars to the registrar, the charge will be void as against the administrator or liquidator. However, an administrator or liquidator appointed after the expiry of the relevant period, is prevented from treating a belatedly registered charge as void. *S95 S400 (2)(b)*

A charge will also be void as against an administrator or liquidator if, at the date of delivery of the particulars, the company is unable to pay its debts or subsequently becomes unable to pay them as a result of the transaction relating to the charge. *S95 S400 (2)(a)*

For these purposes the 'relevant period' is :   S95
                                                                                   S400
                                                                                   (3)(b)
(a)   two years in the case of a floating charge created in favour of a person
         connected with the company (within the meaning of section 249 of the
         IA86), or one year if not so connected; and

(b)   six months in the case of a fixed charge.

The fact that a charge which is registered late is subject to the condition that the
company survives for a given period, may serve unfairly to penalise a mortgagee
whose charge was registered late, although this is likely to be mitigated by the fact
that in practice it is often the chargee who registers the charge. There is a need to
prevent abuse where late registration occurs. However, there is only likely to be
abuse where the company is already insolvent, or on the verge of insolvency and,
for example, the failure to register within the prescribed period was intended to
deceive creditors.

Where the particulars of the charge are delivered for registration and contain   S97
omissions, or are inaccurate, reliance upon the charge is restricted to the rights S402(1)
disclosed in the actual particulars filed and it is void in respect of any undisclosed
rights.

However, the court has the power, on the application of the chargee, to order that S97
the charge will not be void in such circumstances, as against an administrator or   S402(2)
liquidator, or a person who for value acquires an interest or right over property
subject to the charge, where a relevant event occurs at a time when the particulars
are incomplete or inaccurate.

A 'relevant event' in relation to an administrator or liquidator means the   S95
commencement of insolvency proceedings; and in relation to a person acquiring an   S399(2)
interest in or right over property subject to a charge, it means the acquisition of that
interest or right.

Where the court orders that the charge is effective as against an administrator or S97
liquidator of the company, the Act requires the court to be satisfied of certain   S402(4)
matters. In particular, it must be satisfied that the omission or error is unlikely to
prejudice an unsecured creditor to any material extent, or that no person became an
unsecured creditor at a time when the omission or error existed. Only then may it
exercise its discretion to order that the charge is effective as against the
administrator or liquidator.

For the charge to be effective as against a person acquiring an interest in or a right S97
over property, the court must be satisfied that there was no reliance on the   S402(5)
incomplete or inaccurate particulars by that person, in connection with the
acquisition in any relevant respect.

3.2.6   *Memorandum of charge ceasing to affect company's property*

There is no longer a requirement to submit a statutory declaration with the memorandum of satisfaction or release of a charge. Instead, both the company and the chargee are now required to sign, or authorise the signature of, a memorandum of charge, formerly known as a memorandum of satisfaction or release. If either refuses or the chargee is unavailable to sign, the court may order that the memorandum be delivered with only the one signature (see 3.2.5(a) above). The registrar will file in the register the memorandum or, as the case may be, the memorandum signed by or on behalf of one of the parties and an office copy of the court order authorising its delivery. He will then send a copy of the memorandum and of the note evidencing the date of delivery to the company and the chargee. If the memorandum was delivered by any other person interested in the charge, a copy of the memorandum and of the note evidencing the date of delivery will also be sent to that person. `S98 S403 (2)-(4) S103 S417(1)`

Under the 1985 Act, when the charge no longer affected any of the company's property, a statutory declaration, completed by the directors of the company, and a memorandum of satisfaction or release were delivered to the registrar for registration. The effect of submitting the memorandum was that the debt or charge, as the case may be, was to be regarded as satisfied or released. `SS403& 419 CA85`

The significant alteration to the filing requirements is that the Act now requires the chargee to sign the memorandum of charge in respect of all charges. Formerly, only holders of floating charges in Scotland, but not in England or Wales, were required to sign a memorandum of satisfaction or release. Under the 1985 Act, a statutory declaration was capable of being filed fraudulently, e.g. by the company's directors in order to persuade a person to take a charge over assets which appeared to be unencumbered. Apart from the fact that the directors may have been criminally liable in respect of the fraudulent declaration, the effect of this was that the original charge falsely shown as released remained in force and retained priority over subsequent charges. As the memorandum must now be signed by both the company and the chargee, the risk of such abuse must inevitably be reduced.

Where a memorandum is delivered without the debt for which the charge was given being satisfied or the charge being released, the Act provides that the charge is void as against an administrator or liquidator where the relevant event (as defined in 3.2.5(b) above) occurs after the delivery of the memorandum. It is also void as against a person who acquires an interest in, or a right over, property subject to the charge. This reflects the fact that, by signing the memorandum, both the company and the chargee accept that the charge no longer affects the company's property. `S98 S403(5)`

3.2.7   *Additional particulars to be delivered*

The following additional particulars are now required to be delivered to the registrar:

(a)   particulars of the date of the taking up of an issue of debentures and of the amount taken up; and `S100 S408(1)`

(b)   notice of the appointment of a receiver or manager of the property of a   S100
         company registered in England and Wales (the IA86 contains   S409(1)
         corresponding provisions for Scotland).

In addition, the Secretary of State may, by regulations, require notice of the   S100
crystallisation of a floating charge to be given to the registrar. Such regulations   S410
will not extend, however, to floating charges created under Scottish law by a
company registered in Scotland.

3.2.8   Voidness of charges

The Act clarifies the extent and effect of the voidness of charges in certain
circumstances. The new provisions, which are described below, also extend to the
registration of charges by registered oversea companies.

(a)   Subsequent charges

In some circumstances, the Act clarifies the order of precedence between charges   S99
having inconsistent rights. Essentially, a later charge will take precedence over an   S404
earlier charge to the extent that the details of the earlier charge were delivered for
registration late or that the particulars delivered failed to disclose certain rights.

(b)   Restrictions on voidness

A charge is not void as against a person who acquires an interest in or a right over   S99
property where the acquisition is expressly subject to the charge. Similarly, a   S405(1)
charge is not void in relation to any property where a relevant event (see 3.2.5(b)   &(2)
above) occurs after the company, which created the charge, has disposed of the
whole of its interest in that property.

(c)   Effect of exercise of power of sale

Where a charge has become void to any extent by virtue of the provisions   S99
discussed above as against an administrator, liquidator or a person acquiring a   S406(1)
security interest over property subject to the charge, the chargee may sell the   &(2)
property free from the charge. The proceeds of sale are held by the chargee in trust
to be applied, *inter alia*, in discharge of the sums secured by the charge. The
purchaser is not obliged to inquire whether the charge is in fact void.

(d)   Effect of voidness on obligation secured

Where a charge becomes void to any extent by virtue of the 1985 Act provisions on   S99
the registration of charges, the whole of the sum secured by the charge including   S407(1)
any interest is payable on demand.   &(2)

3.3 Copies of instrument and register to be maintained by company

The Act has now brought the provisions applicable to England and Wales into line with those in Scotland so that all companies registered in Great Britain must keep at their registered office a register containing entries of all charges over the property of the company. This means that unlimited companies registered in England and Wales are now required to keep such a register; under the 1985 Act, the requirement only extended to limited companies registered in England and Wales. *S101 S411(2)*

Any person may request the company to provide a copy of any instrument creating or evidencing the charge (whether registrable or not), or of any entry in the register of charges maintained by the company, subject to the payment of a fee. The company must send him the requested copy within ten days after the day on which the request is received or, if later, on which payment is received. If an inspection is refused, or a requested copy of an instrument or entry is not sent within the specified period of ten days, the company and every officer in default is liable to a fine. In addition, the court may, by order, compel an immediate inspection of the register, or direct that the copy be sent immediately. *S101 S412*

In addition, the Secretary of State has been given a power to introduce, by statutory instrument, regulations governing the rights of inspection of any index, register or document that a company is required to maintain under the 1985 Act. *S143(1) S723A*

3.4 Oversea companies

The Act has introduced a new regime for securing the registration in Great Britain of charges on the property of a registered oversea company (a company incorporated in another country but having an established place of business in Great Britain and which has delivered to the registrar certain documents prescribed by the 1985 Act). In relation to companies incorporated overseas, the Act also clarifies that the registration of charges is restricted to companies which are registered oversea companies under the 1985 Act.

3.4.1 More detailed registration requirements

Registered oversea companies are now subject to more detailed registration requirements. The main changes introduced by the Act are as follows:

(a)   registration is required by a registered oversea company where it creates a charge on property which if created by a company registered in Great Britain would require registration under the provisions discussed above; *S105 Sch15 S703B(1)*

(b)   the company must give the registrar the particulars of the charge within 21 days of the date of the charge's creation or the date on which the acquisition of the property subject to a charge was completed; and *Sch15 S703D(2)*

(c)   where the provisions described above do not apply and the property of a   Sch15
        registered oversea company is situated in Great Britain for a continuous   *S703D(3)*
        period of four months and is subject to a charge, the company must
        deliver, if it has not already done so, the prescribed particulars of the
        charge for registration, before the end of the four month period. The
        particulars must be delivered in prescribed form. This will apply, for
        example, if property already subject to a charge is brought to Great Britain.

It appears that future property should be treated as property expected to be situated   Sch15
in Great Britain unless by its very nature this is impossible (such as land abroad).   *S703L(2)*

If an oversea company delivers documents to the registrar, in order to become   Sch15
registered under the 1985 Act, what is the position if at that time, some of its   *S703D(1)*
property is subject to a charge and situated in Great Britain? Alternatively, what if
the charge it created is secured on property expected to be situated in Great Britain
in the future? The answer is the same in both cases. The company must at the time
it delivers the documents, also submit prescribed particulars of the registrable
charges.

Particulars of charges may in all cases be delivered for registration by any person   Sch15
interested in the charge. If a company fails to comply with these new provisions,   *S703D(4)*
and the particulars are not delivered by any other person, the company and every   *&(5)*
officer of it who is in default will be liable to a fine.

3.4.2   *Abolition of the Slavenburg Index*

As a direct consequence of these new provisions, the register maintained by the
registrar and commonly known as the 'Slavenburg Index', is abolished. The Index
arose as a result of the decision of the High Court in *NV Slavenburg's Bank v.
Intercontinental Natural Resources Ltd. 1980 1 All E.R. 955.* In that case, it was
held that the registration of charges provisions applied to foreign companies which
had an established place of business in England and Wales (or Scotland as the case
may be) whether or not they had registered as an oversea company under Part
XXIII of the 1985 Act.

The Index contains an alphabetical list of foreign companies, whether or not
registered under the 1985 Act, which have assets in England or Wales (or Scotland
as the case may be) and have delivered particulars of charges for registration.

The Act has now made it clear that charges are only registrable if created by an   Sch15
oversea company which is registered under the 1985 Act. Therefore, an   *S703A(1)*
unregistered oversea company which has created a charge over assets situated in   *&(3)*
Great Britain will be unable to register particulars of the charge in Great Britain.

The removal of the Index is likely to affect third parties. A person dealing with a
company which is not a registered oversea company can no longer rely on an
inspection of the Index to ascertain whether assets situated in Great Britain are
encumbered. In both cases, assurance as to the unencumbered state of the assets
must be obtained from elsewhere, which as these companies are incorporated
overseas, may not be easy.

3.4.3 Other comments

As mentioned in 3.4.1, a charge must be registered within four months of the assets which are the subject of the charge arriving in Great Britain. The Act has recognised that difficulties may arise with assets such as ships and aircraft, as to whether they are situated in Great Britain for four months. It provides that ships, aircraft and hovercraft are situated in Great Britain if they are registered with the relevant authority in Great Britain. Any other vehicle is situated in Great Britain on a day if, and only if, at any time in that day, its management is directed from a place of business of the company in Great Britain. A vehicle is not regarded as situated in one part of Great Britain only. If an oversea company is registered both in Scotland and in England and Wales, charges over vehicles must therefore be registered in both parts of Great Britain. *Sch15 S703L(1)*

It should be noted that many of the provisions concerning the registration of company charges apply, with appropriate modifications, to charges secured on the property of a registered oversea company. These include the provisions discussed above in 3.2.5, 3.2.6, 3.2.7 and 3.2.8. *Sch15 S703F-J*

4 ANNUAL RETURNS

The Act re-enacts Chapter III of Part XI of the Companies Act 1985. The new provisions modify the basic requirement to deliver annual returns and simplify the existing requirements as to their content. In addition, a new power is inserted enabling the Secretary of State to vary, by regulation, the content of annual returns.

4.1 Return date

A company must deliver successive annual returns made up to a date not later than its 'return date'. The return date is either the anniversary of the company's incorporation, or if the company's last annual return was made up to a different date, the anniversary of that date. Where an annual return is made up to a date prior to the return date, that earlier date will become the return date for the purposes of the following year's annual return. This represents a major change from the delivery requirements under the 1985 Act, under which completion of the annual return was required within 42 days after the annual general meeting. The company also had to deliver a copy of the return 'forthwith' to the registrar. *S139(1) S363(1)*

An annual return must be signed by a director or the secretary of the company (not by both as under the 1985 Act) and delivered to the registrar within 28 days of the date to which it is made up. If a company fails to deliver an annual return within 28 days after the return date or delivers a return which does not contain the prescribed particulars, it is liable to a fine. In the case of continued contravention, there is also a daily default fine. Contravention will continue until the company delivers to the registrar an annual return made up to the return date. Where a company has failed to comply with these provisions every director or secretary of the company will also be liable, unless he can show that he took all reasonable steps to avoid the commission or continuation of the offence. *S139(1) S363 (2)-(4)*

4.2   Additional contents

The Act requires a company to make the following additional disclosures in its annual return:

(a)   the type of company and its principal business activities. Such information may be provided by reference to one or more categories of any prescribed system of classifying such activities;

S139(1)
S364(1)
(b)&(2)

(b)   the date of birth of each individual director of the company (as a consequence of this, the documents delivered by newly-registered companies must give the date of birth of the directors). The 1985 Act required only public companies, or subsidiaries of public companies, to make such disclosures in the return; and

S139(1)
7(2)
Sch19
S364(1)
(e)(i)
1Sch1

(c)   where a private company has elected to dispense with the laying of accounts and reports before the company in general meeting, or with holding an annual general meeting (see 2.2.2 above), a statement to that effect.

S139(1)
S364(1)
(i)

4.3   Deletions

The following information will no longer be required in the annual return:

S139(1)
S364A

(a)   particulars relating to the company's debentures;

(b)   details of the total amount of the company's indebtedness in respect of mortgages and charges; and

(c)   in relation to the share capital, details of non-cash consideration, discounts, calls and share warrants.

The Secretary of State may, by regulation, amend or repeal the provisions dealing with the information required to be disclosed in annual returns.

S139(1)
S365(1)

5   A COMPANY'S OBJECTS AND RELATED MATTERS

The Act has introduced a series of new provisions which deal with the capacity of the company and the related issues of the authority of the board of directors and the rights of third parties. In particular, these changes are concerned with the scope of what a company may lawfully do, the protection of third parties dealing with the company, the duties owed by the directors to their shareholders, and the rights of shareholders in relation to those who exercise power on their behalf.

Prior to the European Communities Act 1972, if a company entered into a contract which was not authorised by the objects clause in its memorandum of association, the contract was void because it was *ultra vires*, or beyond its powers. As a result, the contract could not be enforced by the company even though all the shareholders may have sought to ratify it.

Since then, the effect of the *ultra vires* doctrine has been somewhat restricted by the operation of what has now become section 35 of the 1985 Act which contains the provisions introduced by the European Communities Act 1972. This sought to protect a third party dealing with the company in good faith, by stating that the transaction was deemed to be one which the company had the capacity to make, and that the directors were deemed to have the authority to bind the company.

In 1985, the DTI commissioned Dr. Dan Prentice of Oxford University to advise on the implications of abolishing the *ultra vires* doctrine. His report recommended that the doctrine should be abolished completely. However, the Government has taken the view that total abolition is undesirable, preferring instead to reform the doctrine. As a result, the new provisions introduced by the Act seek to extend the effect of section 35 by abolishing the application of the doctrine to third parties, while retaining it internally by continuing to allow members to bring proceedings to restrain an *ultra vires* act. This gives security to commercial transactions, ensuring that they cannot be called into question once entered into, while retaining the rights of shareholders.

The new legislation, therefore, deals with the following:

(a)   the capacity of a company to enter into transactions and the drafting of the company's constitution so as to broaden its capacity;

(b)   the powers of the directors to bind the company and restrictions on their powers;

(c)   the ability of members of the company to restrain an *ultra vires* act; and

(d)   the protection of third parties entering into contracts.

In addition, because the Government believes that this new regime is not appropriate for charitable companies, there are rules restricting its application to such companies.

5.1   Capacity of company not limited by anything in its memorandum of association

The validity of an act already done by a company is not to be called into question on the grounds that it is beyond the company's capacity. Since a company's capacity is not limited by anything in its memorandum, a completed transaction will have absolute protection from the application of the *ultra vires* rule and, therefore, be valid and enforceable by third parties involved in the transaction. *S108 S35(1)& (2)*

The company may also enforce the transaction. However, where a company intends to enter into a transaction which is beyond its capacity, the Act preserves the right of any member of the company to bring proceedings to restrain the commission of that *ultra vires* act (see 5.6 below).

5.2   Broad objects clauses are acceptable

The Act has relaxed the current approach to drafting objects clauses. At present, a company cannot enter into any transaction of a type not authorised by the objects clause in its memorandum. In order to avoid such restrictions, objects clauses are often drafted so as to permit virtually any transaction and as a result they are frequently very long. This new provision is intended to relieve companies of the need to draft such lengthy objects clauses.

S110(1)
S3A

In future, it will be sufficient for a company's objects clause to state that it 'is to carry on business as a general commercial company'. This will enable a company to carry on any trade or business, including anything incidental, or conducive to, the carrying on of such business. If a company adopts the objects of a 'general commercial company', it will effectively have opted out of the *ultra vires* rule for internal purposes (the rule having been effectively abolished externally in relation to third parties). However, it remains to be seen whether the drafting of the Act is sufficiently wide. For example, it does not refer to the disposal of a business by a general commercial company.

The Act also makes it easier to amend the objects clause. Under the 1985 Act, a company could only alter its objects clause insofar as may be required to enable it to achieve certain specified objectives. The Act dispenses with these requirements and, while preserving the need for a special resolution, provides that the objects clause may be freely amended.

S110(2)
S4(1)

Where the company's objects have been altered, the right of minorities to apply to the court for the cancellation of the alteration is preserved by the Act.

S110(2)
S4(2)

5.3   Power of directors to bind the company

A company's constitution may restrict the authority of directors to bind it in respect of contracts that are otherwise *intra vires*; this is distinct from the doctrine of *ultra vires*, which is concerned with the capacity of the company itself.

The Act, which extends and clarifies the protection offered by the 1985 Act, provides that where a third party deals with the company in good faith (and he is presumed to do so unless the contrary is proved), the power of the board of directors, or persons authorised by them, to bind the company, is deemed to be free of any limitation under the company's constitution. It is now made clear that even those who deal with a company knowing that transactions are beyond the directors' powers are protected. Mere knowledge that the directors are acting beyond their authority will not of itself amount to 'bad faith'. However, the Government has taken the view that bad faith will exist in circumstances where the person dealing with the company is party to a fraud, or assists the directors in abusing their powers.

S108(1)
S35A
(1)&(2)

5.4 Invalidity of certain transactions involving directors

The Act introduces measures designed to prevent the new provisions from being used as a vehicle for fraud by addressing those situations where the directors have exceeded any limitation placed upon their powers to bind the company, and where the parties to the transaction include a director of the company or its holding company, or a person connected with, or a company associated with, such a director. In such circumstances the transaction is voidable at the instance of the company. *S109(1) S322A(1) &(2)*

Regardless of whether or not the transaction is avoided, any director who is a party, a person connected with him or any director who authorised the transaction, is liable: *S109(1) S322A(3)*

(a)   to account to the company for any gain made directly or indirectly from the transaction; and

(b)   to indemnify the company for any loss or damage resulting from the transaction.

For these purposes, the definition of 'connected person' under the 1985 Act, will apply, so that it will include a director's spouse, child, partner or a body corporate in which a director has a significant (usually over 20%) holding. *S346 CA85*

Such persons will not be liable if they can show that at the time of the transaction they were unaware that the directors were exceeding their powers. *S109(1) S322A(6)*

The transaction will cease to be voidable where: *S109(1) S322A(5)*

(a)   restitution of any money or other asset, being the subject-matter of the transaction, is no longer possible;

(b)   the company is indemnified for any loss or damage resulting from the transaction;

(c)   the avoidance would affect a person acquiring rights in good faith and who was unaware that the directors had exceeded their powers; or

(d)   the transaction is ratified by the appropriate resolution of the company in general meeting.

It is important to note that persons who are not directors of the company but who are involved in the transaction are unaffected by these measures. Instead, their position continues to be governed by the general provisions discussed in 5.1 and 5.3 above. Moreover, a court may grant severance of the transaction to protect such other parties where they dealt with the company in good faith. *S109(1) S322A (7)*

As previously mentioned, this section is intended to prevent directors acting in a fraudulent manner. For example, a dishonest director could easily misuse his power to bind the company to a transaction from which he is to benefit. The fact that a transaction is voidable at the instance of the company will enable a company to recover property or other monies which had been transferred fraudulently under the transaction.

5.5   No duty on third parties to enquire as to capacity or authority

The Act has made it clear that a party to a transaction with the company is not bound to enquire as to whether the transaction is permitted by the memorandum of the company or as to any limitations on the authority of its board of directors. *S108(1) S35B*

This clarification has important ramifications for a doctrine closely connected to that of *ultra vires*, the doctrine of deemed (or constructive) notice. Under this doctrine, a person is deemed to have notice of the details disclosed in any document kept at Companies House or made available for inspection by the company. The fact that persons who deal with a company need no longer enquire as to capacity or authority, will inevitably serve to curtail the application of the doctrine of deemed notice. In order to correspond with the overall package of reform, the Act has abolished the doctrine of deemed notice for almost all purposes (see 6.3 below).

5.6   Ability of company members to restrain or ratify an *ultra vires* act

The existing right of any member of the company to bring proceedings to restrain the doing of an act which is beyond the capacity of the company, or the powers of the directors, is preserved by the Act. However, it has restricted their rights in one direction. Where a company is required to carry out an *ultra vires* act in pursuance of a legal obligation arising from a previous act of the company, the Act allows the company to proceed and prohibits any member of the company from instituting proceedings to restrain the commission of that act. This evidences the Government's intention to provide security for commercial transactions previously entered into. However, the right of a member of the company to bring proceedings against one or more of the directors, who had incurred liability by reason of an earlier act of the company, or its directors, is unaffected. *S108(1) SS35(2) &(3)& 35A(4) &(5)*

Companies have always been able to ratify acts where the limitations on the authority of their directors have been exceeded. However, the power to ratify was not available in respect of acts which were *ultra vires*. This restriction no longer applies and such acts may be ratified by the company by special resolution. *S108(1) S35(3)*

The effect of a failure to ratify is that the transaction entered into will still be valid *vis-a-vis* third parties dealing with the company in good faith, although unenforceable by the company against such third parties. Despite this, a member may still sue the directors in respect of any liability incurred in relation to that act of the company. The company may, however, pass a further special resolution for the sole purpose of relieving the directors of such liability.

The retention of the 'internal' operation of the *ultra vires* rule is regarded by the Government as an important safeguard for shareholders which they ought to be able to keep in place if they so choose (however, see 5.2 above).

5.7 Charitable companies

The extent of the reform of the *ultra vires* doctrine has been restricted in the case of charitable companies. In view of their specialised purpose, it is considered inappropriate to offer them the same latitude as has been extended to other companies and therefore a special regime has been constructed for such companies. SS111&
112
SS30-
30C
ChA60

In particular, an *ultra vires* transaction will not be enforceable against a company which is a charity by a person who is aware of its charitable status. Accordingly, there is a new requirement for any charitable company which does not have the words 'charity' or 'charitable' in its name to state that it is a charity on all letters, notices and other business stationery. S111(1)
S30B
&30C
ChA60

6 OTHER ADMINISTRATIVE MATTER

6.1 Disclosure of interests in shares

Part VI of the 1985 Act requires persons who have acquired an interest in shares in a public company to notify that interest to the company concerned within 5 business days, where it represents 5 per cent. of the company's relevant share capital. The 'relevant share capital' refers essentially to the company's issued share capital and, in particular, to classes of shares which carry rights to vote in all circumstances at general meetings of the company.

The Act has amended the 1985 Act, by reducing the notifiable percentage from 5 per cent. to 3 per cent. Furthermore, the period within which the company must be notified of the interest has been reduced from 5 business days to 2 business days. These changes have been introduced in an effort to increase market transparency and, therefore, to make it more difficult for purchasers of a company's shares to build up a secret stake in the company. S134(1)-
(3)
SS199(2)
202(1)
(4)&
206(8)

There is also a new requirement that the notification to the company must differentiate between the number of shares and the number of rights to acquire shares, such as interests in options or convertible securities. This will have the effect of requiring a major shareholder which has exercised such a right to notify the company that it has done so. This closes a perceived loophole in the previous rules, which required rights to acquire shares to be taken into account when determining the existence of a disclosable interest but did not require the exercise of such rights to be notified. S134(4)
S202(3)

The Secretary of State is also granted a power to further change these limits by regulation. He will, therefore, be in a position to act relatively quickly to make further amendments should the above changes to the disclosure requirements prove to be ineffective. S134(5)
S210A

6.2 Companies House records and related matters

The Act has extended the existing provisions relating to the delivery of documents to the registrar, their storage by him and their retrieval for the purposes of public inspection. This is intended to improve the efficiency and effectiveness of

Companies House by broadening the existing provisions to take account of the electronic transmission of information and the development of new technologies.

All documents delivered to the registrar must meet any requirements prescribed in regulations or specified by the registrar in order to allow them to be read (in the case of non-legible documents such as microfilm) and copied. They must also show prominently the registered number of the company to which they relate. In this context, 'document' includes information recorded in any form and 'legible' means capable of being read with the naked eye.

S125(1)
S706
S125(2)
S707
S127(1)
S715A(1)

Information contained in a document delivered to the registrar may be kept by him in whatever form he thinks fit as long as it is possible to inspect the information and produce a copy of it in legible form. However, the registrar must also keep the original documents for at least ten years, after which he may destroy them.

S126
*S707A
(1)&(2)*

6.3   Abolition of doctrine of deemed notice

The doctrine of deemed (or constructive) notice has been abolished by the Act. The doctrine as it applied to companies, originally developed as a constitutional doctrine, applicable only to the memorandum and articles and particulars of directors. It was later extended by case law to special resolutions and the registration of company charges. Prior to the Act, the doctrine had the effect that a member of the public was deemed to have notice of any matter disclosed in any official company document kept at the company's registered office, or filed with Companies House. However, it should be noted that section 35 of the 1985 Act has already restricted its application (see 5.5 above).

The effect of abolishing the doctrine is that, subject to certain exceptions (see below), a person shall not be taken to have notice of any matter merely because it is disclosed in any document made available for inspection by the registrar of companies, or by a company. For these purposes, 'document' includes any material which contains information.

S142
*S711A(1)
&(3)*

Nevertheless, a person cannot rely on the fact that he did not have notice of certain matters if he failed to make such enquiries as ought reasonably to be made in the circumstances. The circumstances in which it would be reasonable for a person not to inspect documents kept at the company's registered office (or at Companies House), are unclear.

S142
S711A(2)

The abolition of the doctrine will not affect:

S142
S711A(4)

(a)   section 416 of the 1985 Act under which a person taking a charge over a company's property is deemed to have notice of any matter requiring registration and disclosed on the register of charges at the time the charge was created (see 3.2.4 above); or

(b)   the registration of land charges under section 198 of the Law of Property Act 1925, as it applies by virtue of section 3(7) of the Land Charges Act 1972. In relation to land charges over property in England and Wales, registration will continue to be deemed to constitute actual notice of the instrument or matter, to all persons and for all purposes connected with the land affected.

6.4   A company's registered office

The Act has re-enacted, with modifications, the existing provisions relating to a company's registered office and clarifies certain matters that were previously unclear.

It is now clear that a change in the registered office takes effect from the time that due notice of that fact has been delivered to the registrar and entered on the register. This ensures that a person can at all times determine the whereabouts of the company's registered office. This will be important, for example, in a case where a document needs to be properly served on the company. S136 *S287(4)*

A company is required to keep various registers at its registered office and a failure to do so is a criminal offence. Problems might therefore occur where a company changes its registered office and moves its registers to the new registered office. The precise date on which the location of the new registered office is registered will not be known to the company without it making a specific inquiry at Companies House. To avoid a company inadvertently committing a criminal offence, the Act gives protection to a company as long as it moves its registers to the new registered office within 14 days of giving notice of the change. During this 14 day period process may still be served at the former registered office. Similarly, if the registers are moved and it is not practicable to give prior notice, no offence is committed if notice of the change is given within 14 days. S136 *S287(4)- (6)*

6.5   Company contracts and execution of documents by companies

In addition to simplifying the provisions under the 1985 Act relating to the form of company contracts in England and Wales, the Act has introduced new provisions dealing with the execution of documents by a company.

6.5.1   *Execution of documents: England and Wales*

A document is executed by a company by the affixing of its common seal. However, there is now no requirement for a company to have a common seal and a document signed by both a director and the secretary of the company, or by two directors of the company, and expressed to be executed by the company, will have the same effect as if it were under seal. S130(1) *S36A (2)-(4)*

A document executed in this way, which is intended by the persons making it to be a deed, and if that fact is clear on its face, will take effect on delivery as a deed. If such a document is signed by persons purporting to be a director and secretary of the company, but who in fact are not, the Act seeks to protect a *bona fide* purchaser by providing that the document is deemed to have been properly executed. S130(1) *S36A (5)&(6)*

The aim of this provision is to reduce the unnecessary burden placed upon companies to use a seal in certain situations. The Act does not, however, prohibit a company from continuing to use its company seal as before. It merely relieves the company of the obligation to use it.

6.5.2   *Execution of documents: Scotland*

The abolition of the requirement that a company should have a common seal also extends to Scotland. As a result, there are new provisions which, under the law of Scotland, have effect with respect to the signing and subscription of documents by persons acting on behalf of a company. The effect of these is that documents can generally be executed without being sealed. *S130(3) S36B*

6.6   Financial assistance for purposes of employees' share scheme

The Act has widened the scope for companies to give financial assistance for the purposes of employees' share schemes, thereby encouraging the spread of wider individual share ownership (see also 6.7 below). Under the 1985 Act, the only form of financial assistance not prohibited in connection with such schemes was the provision by a company of money for the acquisition of fully paid up shares in itself or its holding company.

The Act permits any form of financial assistance as long as it is provided in good faith. For example, companies will be able to repay some or all of the capital or interest on sums borrowed in connection with such schemes, or give guarantees, or some other form of security or indemnity, to banks who lend money to employees' share schemes. *S132 S153 (4)(b)*

6.7   Partnership companies

During the passage of the Act through Parliament, the Government accepted the principle of an amendment, the aim of which was to make it easier to set up partnership companies. The Government sees partnership companies as a means of furthering its aim of wider individual share ownership. A partnership company is defined in the Act as '..a company limited by shares whose shares are intended to be held to a substantial extent by or on behalf of its employees.' *S128 S8A(1)*

The Act allows the Secretary of State to prescribe, by regulations, a model set of articles of association appropriate for partnership companies, known as *Table G*. Companies limited by shares may adopt the whole or any part of *Table G* as their articles, just as companies at present adopt in whole, or in part, the provisions of *Table A*. As is the case with *Table A*, any subsequent alteration to *Table G* will not affect a company which had adopted (in whole or in part) the Table before the alteration took place. *S128 S8A (1)-(3)*

6.8 Effecting of insurance for officers and auditors of company

The Act has relaxed the effect of section 310 of the 1985 Act by enabling companies to purchase and maintain for any of their officers or auditors, insurance against liability for negligence, default, breach of duty or breach of trust. Under the 1985 Act, companies were prevented from indemnifying their officers and auditors against liability. As paying for insurance on behalf of such persons amounted to just that, it was doubtful whether such insurance had any effect. *S137(1) S310(3) (a)*

Where a company takes out insurance on behalf of its officers or auditors, that fact must be disclosed in the directors' report . *S137(2) 5ASch7*

6.9 Directors' transactions

The Act has increased the monetary limits on certain exemptions which permit loans to directors (and similar transactions) of small amounts. The limit on short-term quasi-loans to directors is increased from £1,000 to £5,000 and the limit on loans to directors of small amounts is increased from £2,500 to £5,000. With regard to loans or quasi-loans made by money lending companies to their directors, the limit is increased from £50,000 to £100,000. *S138 SS332(1) (b),334& 338(4)& (6)*

6.10 Members' rights to damages

The Act has introduced a new clause which provides that a person is not prevented from bringing an action claiming damages against a company in which he holds shares. The effect of this is to abolish the rule in *Houldsworth v. City of Glasgow Bank (1880) 5 App Cas 317*. Essentially, the rule provided that a subscriber of shares in a company, who remains a member of the company, cannot claim damages for misrepresentation or breach of the contract of allotment against the company unless he first rescinds that contract. The courts will now have the freedom to consider the facts of each case and to apply the appropriate remedies. *S131 S111A*

6.11 Membership of holding company

The previous prohibition on subsidiaries being members of their holding companies is replaced by similar new rules which clarify the status of prior holdings (i.e. those acquired by a company in another company which subsequently becomes its holding company). These are at present illegal but no consequences flow from this because the present rules fail to deal with prior holdings. The new prohibition permits them to remain (and they may be added to by way of bonus shares) but no voting rights may be exercised in respect of them. There is no restriction on the payment of dividend on such shares. The prohibition on being a member of the holding company does not apply if the subsidiary is concerned only as a market maker. *S129 S23*

6.12 Issue of redeemable shares

The terms of redemption must be specified at or before the time any redeemable shares are issued. *S133 S159(A)*

Chapter 5

Auditors

1 SUMMARY

Part II of the Act is concerned with the regulation and qualification of auditors. Principally, it introduces the EC Eighth Directive into UK legislation. However, the Government has also taken the opportunity to change some of the other aspects of the law relating to auditors and to partnerships.

Previously, a company's auditor has had to be a member of one of the four bodies of accountants recognised for this purpose by the Secretary of State (unless he was someone who was individually authorised, usually as the holder of an equivalent overseas qualification) but the profession has otherwise been entirely self-regulating. The new legislation changes this; the Directive requires that statutory audits may only be performed by persons who are approved by the authorities of the member states. In the UK, the authority to give such approval will be delegated to supervisory bodies approved by the Secretary of State. In practice these are likely to be the existing professional bodies governing auditors, but they will now be subject to detailed legal requirements which will have to be embodied in their own rules.

In line with the requirement that all auditors be approved, there will be registers of all approved auditors. The Act has also removed the prohibition on an incorporated firm being appointed auditor of a company, and made various other amendments relating to the legal position of partnerships.

In addition, legislation relating to the appointment, resignation and removal of auditors has been amended. This is partly a result of introducing the elective regime for private companies, although the law has been redrafted and rationalised in other respects as well.

2   SUPERVISORY   BODIES   AND   PROFESSIONAL QUALIFICATIONS

Two types of supervisory body are to be established under the Act:

(a)   Recognised Supervisory Bodies (RSBs), of which all company auditors must be members. These are described in 2.1 and 2.2 below; and

(b)   Recognised Qualifying Bodies (RQBs), which will offer the appropriate professional qualification which is a prerequisite of membership of a RSB. These, and the details of the qualifications that they will offer are described in 2.3 below.

The same organisation can be both a RSB and a RQB and the existing professional bodies governing auditors are likely to fulfil both functions.

At present, an auditor must be individually authorised by the Secretary of State or be a member of The Institute of Chartered Accountants in England and Wales, The Institute of Chartered Accountants of Scotland, The Institute of Chartered Accountants in Ireland (the Institutes) or of The Chartered Association of Certified Accountants (CACA). Under the new Act, the auditor will have to be a member of a RSB and be eligible under its rules for appointment. This membership rule also applies to persons whose overseas qualifications are approved by the Secretary of State (see 2.3.4).   `S25(1) (a)&(b) S389(1) (a)&(3) CA85 (rep)`

2.1   Recognition of RSBs

Each RSB is to be: `S30(1)`

'...a body established in the United Kingdom (whether a body corporate or an unincorporated association) which maintains and enforces rules as to:

(a)   the eligibility of persons seeking appointment as company auditors; and

(b)   the conduct of company audit work,

which are binding on persons seeking appointment or acting as company auditors either because they are members of that body or because they are otherwise subject to its control.'

Bodies wishing to be RSBs must apply to the Secretary of State for recognition. The conditions for the grant and revocation of recognition are given in Schedule 11 to the Act. Prospective RSBs must submit their rules and any other written guidance, while providing the Secretary of State with any other information that he may reasonably require. The Schedule gives the Secretary of State the right to refuse to recognise a body if he considers that its recognition is unnecessary bearing in mind that there are other bodies controlling the profession which have been, or are likely to be, authorised. Accordingly, the DTI need only recognise the existing professional bodies.   `1&2(3) Sch 11`

2.2 Required rules, practices and arrangements of supervisory bodies

To some extent, the requirements simply formalise the existing situation. Members of the Institutes and CACA are already required to act in accordance with their rules which are enforced by their disciplinary committees. However, the RSBs will be required to introduce procedures to maintain the competence of their members and to monitor and enforce compliance with the rules, which are likely to be much more extensive than those applied at present by the professional bodies.

2.2.1 Eligibility for appointment as auditor

RSBs must ensure that the following persons only are eligible for appointment as company auditor: 4(1) Sch11

(a)   individuals who hold appropriate qualifications; and

(b)   firms controlled by qualified persons.

2.2.2 Fit and proper persons

The rules and practices of the RSB must be such that only 'fit and proper' persons are appointed as company auditors. This follows the terminology that is used in the IA86, and the Insolvency Practitioners' Regulations detail a number of matters that are to be taken into account in determining whether someone is 'fit and proper'. The RSB has to take into account the person's professional conduct, including the conduct of employees and some other close business associates. The meaning of 'associates' for this purpose depends on whether the person is an individual, body corporate or partnership. S52 6Sch11 R4SI1986/ 1992

2.2.3 Professional integrity and independence

The RSBs' rules must ensure that company audit work is conducted properly and with integrity. This phrase is based on the Eighth Directive's requirement that audits be carried out with 'professional integrity', but its meaning is not further defined. The DTI, in its consultative document on the implementation of the Directive, considered that this meant that the rules must address two distinct areas: firstly, the standards of performance of the audit, including compliance with approved auditing standards and guidelines and secondly, the more general ethical standards that members will have to abide by, such as rules to cover independence, objectivity, integrity and client confidentiality. 7Sch11

2.2.4 Technical standards

The technical standards and the way in which they are to be applied in practice to company audits must be the subject of RSB rules. Again, the precise meaning is unclear but it appears to be a reference to the need for auditing standards and guidelines, rather than statements of standard accounting practice. 8Sch11

2.2.5   Procedures for maintaining competence

The rules and practices of the RSB must ensure that eligible persons continue to   9Sch11
maintain 'an appropriate level of competence' in the conduct of company audits.

There has been some controversy about whether such rules are a requirement of the
Directive. The Government, however, believes that it cannot be implemented
properly without such procedures; it believes that it is essential that the accountancy
profession ensures that its members remain up-to-date and, accordingly, that this is
an area in which the RSBs will have to introduce additional regulation.

2.2.6   Enforcement and investigation

The RSBs' rules must include adequate provisions in respect of:

(a)   monitoring and enforcement of compliance with the rules;   10Sch11

(b)   admission and expulsion of members; grant and withdrawal of eligibility   11Sch11
           for appointment as company auditor; and disciplinary procedures. These
           rules must be 'fair and reasonable' and there must be an adequate appeals
           procedure;

(c)   the investigation of complaints against its members and arising out of its   12Sch11
           own activities as a RSB; and

(d)   ensuring that company auditors have sufficient professional indemnity   13Sch11
           insurance or other appropriate arrangements to meet claims arising from
           company audit work.

The first of these, monitoring and enforcing compliance, is the subject of some
debate. 'Monitoring' may imply an active, regular examination of the activities of a
profession comprising many thousands of audit firms and individuals. The rules
will be made after consultation between the bodies and the DTI.

2.2.7   Exemption of the RSBs from liability for damages

The RSBs and their officers, employees and members of their governing bodies are   S48(1)
exempted from damages in respect of any action or omission following from the
exercise of their statutory duties, unless it can be shown that they have acted in bad
faith. This is because the legislation requires the RSBs to ensure the compliance of
members and member firms with all of the rules. Without any limitation on their
liability, RSBs might find it difficult to take the decisions necessitated by their
supervisory role; they might also be in danger of being joined in any action taken
against auditors for negligence.

2.2.8   RSBs, restrictive practices and competition law

The Act introduces a requirement that the RSBs' rules and other guidance be   S47
submitted to the Director General of Fair Trading (DGFT) before recognition is   1Sch14

granted in order that he may determine whether they will restrict, distort or prevent competition. The Secretary of State will not make a recognition order unless it appears that any restriction is reasonably justifiable in the light of the purposes of the Act.

2.3 Qualifications and recognised qualifying bodies

The Act makes it a requirement of the law that auditors hold an 'appropriate qualification'. It defines the educational level of entrants to the profession and the duration of their training, while the contents of the theoretical training that must be followed will be introduced by statutory instrument at a later date. Bodies offering qualifications must be approved by the Secretary of State. There are also provisions to enable those otherwise unqualified individuals with an authorisation under the 1967 Act to continue to act as auditors of unquoted companies.

2.3.1 Appropriate qualifications

A person will hold an appropriate qualification if he falls into one of the following categories: S31(1)

(a) he satisfied the existing criteria for appointment as an auditor under the 1985 Act by being a member of one of the bodies recognised under section 389(1)(a), immediately before January 1,1990 and immediately before the commencement of section 25 of the Act which redefines eligibility. This is a transitional arrangement to protect those who have already qualified at the time of the Act ;

(b) he holds a recognised professional qualification obtained in the UK (this will, in future, be the 'appropriate qualification' for all new auditors);

(c) he holds an approved overseas qualification and satisfies any additional requirements that have been set down by the Secretary of State (see 2.3.4 below).

There are also provisions for others whose qualification for appointment did not depend on their membership of the bodies recognised under section 389(1)(a) of the 1985 Act, which principally includes those persons who have received individual authorisation under section 389(1)(b) on the basis of qualifications obtained outside the UK. They have a twelve month period in which to notify the Secretary of State that they wish to continue to be treated as qualified. This is to enable the DTI to establish how many of them are still in practice. In order to continue in practice, these auditors, like all others, will have to become members of a RSB. S31 (2)-(4)

In addition, students who have commenced their training before January 1,1990 and who qualify before January 1,1996 will also be treated as holding an appropriate qualification as long as their training is approved for this purpose by the Secretary of State. S31(5)

2.3.2   Recognised qualifying body

In order to offer recognised professional qualifications, bodies must be approved
by the Secretary of State. The procedure for authorisation is comparable to that for
recognition as a RSB. Conditions for the grant and revocation of recognition are
given in Schedule 12 to the Act. The body offering the qualification must have
rules and arrangements sufficient to ensure compliance with the various entry,
examination and training requirements which are summarised below.

S32
9Sch12

2.3.3   Conditions for qualification

The qualification must only be open to persons who have attained university
entrance level (without necessarily having gone to university) or have a sufficient
period of professional experience. In order to satisfy the latter criterion, a person
must have had at least seven years' experience in a professional capacity in finance,
law and accountancy. Periods of theoretical instruction, up to a maximum of four
years, can count towards the necessary experience as long as the instruction lasts
for at least one year and is attested by an examination recognised for this purpose
by the Secretary of State.

4&6
Sch12

Those who seek recognition must pass an examination, which tests theoretical
knowledge and the ability to apply it in practice, and have completed at least three
years' practical training. Persons may be exempted from examination in subjects in
which they already hold a recognised qualification (in the main, having passed a
university examination of equivalent standard or obtained a degree in that subject);
similarly, approved diplomas evidencing practical training may exempt a person
from the requirement to demonstrate the practical application of his theoretical
knowledge.

7(1)-(3)
&8(1)
Sch12

The subjects are not named in the Act; the Secretary of State is to define them by
statutory instrument. However, the content of the theoretical training is defined by
the Directive and is in line with that presently prescribed by the professional
bodies.

7(4)
Sch12

The practical training must be given by persons approved by a RQB as being
suitable and at least two thirds of it must be with a fully-qualified auditor. A
'substantial part' (not defined) of the training must be in company audit work or
other audit work approved by the Secretary of State as being of a similar nature
(for example, a building society audit would probably suffice).

8Sch12

2.3.4   Approval of overseas qualifications

In this area, the Act reflects more than the requirements of the Eighth Directive; it
also takes into account the previous legislation in the 1985 Act and the regime
introduced by the Mutual Recognition Directive which will regulate the recognition
by member states of each other's professional qualifications. In essence, member
states may not refuse access to a regulated profession to a national of another
member state already holding the required certificate. Where a professional activity

requires a precise knowledge of national law, however, and the provision of advice and assistance concerning it is an essential feature of the activity, the member state may introduce either an adaptation period or an aptitude test. In addition, of course, the new legislation must make provision for nationals of non-EC countries.

The Secretary of State is empowered to consider a professional qualification obtained outside the UK as 'approved'. This will only happen if he is satisfied that it gives a degree of professional competence equivalent to a recognised professional qualification. Persons with such qualifications may be required to obtain additional educational qualifications in order to demonstrate that they have a sufficient knowledge of UK law and practice. There is a reciprocity provision, in that the Secretary of State is not required to recognise a qualification unless the other country also recognises UK qualifications. *S33 (1)-(4)*

2.4 Requirement to set up registers

The Directive requires the RSBs to maintain an up-to-date list of approved auditors, whether they be firms or individuals. This list must be made available to the public. Many of the details regarding the register are to yet to be established and will be introduced by statutory instrument after consultation between the professional bodies and the DTI. It is clear that the register must identify those qualified individuals who are responsible for company audit work on behalf of firms. The regulations will require that the register includes the names and addresses and the RSB to which individuals and firms belong. There will also have to be a register of the directors and shareholders in bodies corporate and partners in partnerships, together with their respective addresses. *S35 (1)&(2) S36 (1)&(2)*

2.5 Fees

Furthering the Government's view that regulations such as these should, if possible, result in no net cost to the Government, the Secretary of State is given the power to introduce a statutory instrument to require both initial and periodical fees from RSBs and RQBs. *S45 (1)-(5)*

2.6 Reserve powers to delegate functions

The Act empowers the Secretary of State, if he so wishes, to establish a body corporate which can exercise any of his functions under Part II of the Act. It seems that the Government sees this as a reserve provision and that any such body would be concerned with the administration and regulation of auditors. *S46*

3 ELIGIBILITY FOR APPOINTMENT AS COMPANY AUDITOR

As described in 2 above, the main prerequisite for qualification to act as a company auditor will be membership of a RSB. However, there are various other aspects of eligibility dealt with in the Act.

3.1   Eligibility of partnerships and corporate bodies.

The Act provides that an individual or a firm (defined to mean either a body corporate or a partnership) may be appointed company auditor. Formerly it was not possible for an auditor to be a corporate body. However, a number of EC countries already permit audits to be performed by companies. In addition, in the UK, incorporation is seen by some as a partial answer to the problem of professional liability in that it would limit the liability of individuals (although not that of the audit company) in professional indemnity claims. Therefore, this prohibition has been repealed. S25(2) S389(6) CA85 (rep)

Firms may only perform statutory audits if they are controlled by qualified persons; 'control' is defined in terms of the power to make decisions. The legislation covers various forms of internal organisation so as to ensure that, whatever form of constitution an eligible firm has, a majority of those who make the decisions will be qualified persons. A 'qualified person' is one who holds an appropriate qualification, as discussed in 2.3.1 above. 4(1)(b)(ii) &5 Sch11

3.2   Effect of appointment of partnerships

The Act has cleared up various anomalies in the previous company legislation with regard to the appointment of partnerships as auditors. Strictly, under English law, appointment was of individuals, not partnerships. As noted above, the Act now provides that partnerships may be appointed; it clarifies the fact that the appointment is of the partnership itself and not the partners and that the appointment will continue despite the routine cessations of partnerships when members join and leave. The situation has always been different in Scotland where partnerships have separate legal personality. S26(1)& (2)

Where a partnership ceases, the appointment may go to any eligible partnership that succeeds to the practice or any individual who was previously a member of the partnership and has taken over the practice. Succession, for these purposes, applies only if substantially all of the members of the successor partnership are the same as before or, in the case of an individual, he has taken over substantially all of the business. S26(3) &(4)

If there is no 'succession' as defined, for example in the case of the merger of accountancy firms, the appointment may extend, with the the consent of the company concerned, to the partnership or individual who takes over all or an agreed part of the business. S26(5)

3.3   Ineligibility due to lack of independence

It is still the case that a person is ineligible to be a company's auditor if he is an officer or employee of the company, or a partner or employee of such a person. The Act adds an extra condition: he will be ineligible if he is insufficiently independent of the company. Lack of independence will be defined by statutory instrument after further consultation with the professional bodies. S389(6) (a)&(b) CA85rep S27(1), (2)&(4)

3.3.1   *Incorporation and independence*

There are two main issues where the auditor is a corporate body:

(a)   control over the decision-making processes within incorporated audit firms; and

(b)   share ownership, of the shares in the firms themselves, and ownership by them of shares in other companies.

The first of these was mentioned at 3.1 above, and the Act lays down certain detailed rules. It is probable that more stringent rules will be laid down by the RSBs themselves, in all likelihood for partnerships as well as for incorporated bodies. 7Sch11

Share ownership of the auditor company is not addressed directly by the legislation, although RSBs are required to have rules preventing individuals who do not hold an appropriate qualification from exerting an influence over the conduct of audits in such a way as to compromise their integrity or independence.

The likelihood is that separate limits will be laid down on the shareholding rights of non-auditors (those who work for audit firms as employees or directors but are not themselves auditors) and outsiders (persons unconnected other than as shareholders), with the aggregate of such holdings being less than 50% of the total shares. Outsiders may, unlike non-auditors, be prohibited from holding shares that carry voting rights although firms may be permitted to appoint non-shareholding outsiders as non-executive directors. Non-auditors would be permitted to hold a proportion of the places on the board of directors. It is also probable that there will be a blanket prohibition against an audit company auditing any other company in which it holds shares or which holds shares in it. This prohibition will cover fellow group companies on both sides and may even extend to associated enterprises.

3.3.2   *Other issues*

The Act gives the Secretary of State the power to introduce a statutory instrument making mandatory the separate disclosure of fees for audit and non-audit services; this is discussed in Chapter 2 at 2.4. This is because of the perceived compromise to independence created by the provision of non-audit services to audit clients. Some member states, for example France, go further and forbid auditors to perform such services. There is no proposal at present to move towards this position in the UK.

The professional bodies have always recognised that, in order properly to perform their duties, auditors must be truly independent of their clients and that there are a number of areas in which this independence could be compromised. The existing rules on independence are likely to be retained. Therefore, for example, the RSBs' rules are likely to continue to prevent auditors from owning shares in, or obtaining loans from, client companies. There will also be rules governing the proportion of fee income that a partnership may obtain from a single client and prohibiting an auditor from making executive decisions in client companies.

3.4   Appointment of an ineligible auditor

If an auditor ceases to be eligible under the rules of the RSB to which he belongs   SS28&29
he must vacate his office immediately, giving notice in writing to the company. If he acts when ineligible the Secretary of State may direct the company to retain another auditor (eligible for appointment with that company) to carry out a second audit or to review the first audit, stating (with reasons) whether a second audit is required. The Act provides that the costs of the review and second audit may be recovered from an auditor who continues to act while knowing himself to be ineligible.

This section appears to have been drafted to cover ineligibility due to lack of independence. An auditor could also cease to be eligible as a result of disciplinary action resulting in expulsion from a RSB or, in the case of a firm, if its eligibility for appointment as a company auditor was withdrawn.

4   OTHER AMENDMENTS

4.1.   Appointment, resignation and removal of auditors

The Act has amended various sections relating to the appointment, resignation and removal of auditors.

4.1.1   *Effects of the introduction of the elective regime for private companies*

The procedures which have been introduced by the Act, which enable private companies to dispense with or modify certain procedural requirements, are dealt with in general in Chapter 4 at 2.2.2. There are two elections that may affect the auditors:

(a)   a company may elect to dispense with the annual appointment of auditors; and

(b)   a company may elect not to lay accounts before the members in general meeting but without making the election in (a). Under the 1985 Act, auditors are to be appointed at every meeting at which accounts are laid. Therefore, there has to be a new mechanism to deal with the appointment of auditors.

If a company makes the election in (a) then the auditors shall be deemed to be   S119(1)
reappointed annually for as long as the election remains in force.   *S386*

During this time, any member may give notice in writing to the company proposing that the auditors' appointment be brought to an end; the directors must convene a general meeting to decide the issue. This must be held within 28 days of the notice being given.

S122(1)
S393

If the company makes the election not to lay accounts before the members in general meeting but without also making the election discussed in the preceding paragraph, it must still hold a general meeting each year for the purpose of re-electing the auditors. This meeting must be held within 28 days of the despatch to the members of the accounts; this period after the despatch of the accounts is defined as the 'time for appointing auditors'. The auditors so appointed will remain in office until the end of the time for appointing auditors in the subsequent financial year. There are also rules that cover circumstances in which the members require the accounts to be laid in general meeting and for the appointment of the first auditors by the directors.

S119(1)
S385A

4.1.2 Statements on ceasing to be auditor

Under the 1985 Act, an auditor's resignation is not effective unless it contains a statement of any circumstances connected with the resignation that he considers should be brought to the notice of the members or creditors of the company, or a statement that there are none. This now applies when an auditor ceases to hold the position for whatever reason, so it will also include circumstances when an auditor is removed by the members or is not reappointed by them in general meeting.

S123(1)
S394

Chapter 6

Takeovers and mergers

1 SUMMARY

The Act amends the provisions of the Fair Trading Act 1973 (FTA73) which deal with takeovers and mergers, introducing certain new provisions which supplement the present merger legislation. There is a new voluntary pre-notification system, providing a formal procedure by which a merger proposal may be cleared in advance of the bid proceeding. This will be of particular use in the majority of cases, where no competition or other concerns arise. This procedure is discussed at 2 below.

Where a proposed merger raises competition issues, these can often be resolved by selling part of the merged business. The Act allows the Secretary of State to accept and enforce undertakings given by the merging parties, under which they promise to divest certain parts of the merged business in order to avoid having the merger referred to the Monopolies and Mergers Commission (MMC) (see 3 below).

There are also new provisions designed to restrict a party from acquiring shares in the other party to the merger, at a time when the merger has been referred to the MMC and to allow the Secretary of State to recover the costs of merger control. Minor changes are also made to improve procedures and remedy existing deficiencies in merger and related competition legislation.

At present, the process of referring a merger under the FTA73 consists of a number of stages which may be summarised as follows. In the course of its policing function, the Office of Fair Trading (OFT) identifies proposed mergers. If the particular merger is thought likely to have a detrimental impact on the public interest, the OFT will carry out an initial investigation. This investigation is designed to determine whether the merger amounts to a 'merger situation qualifying for investigation' and, if so, whether there are sufficient reasons for seeking an investigation by the MMC. Briefly, a merger situation qualifying for investigation may arise in two circumstances. Firstly, where the merger creates or enhances, or is likely to create or enhance, a monopoly situation amounting to a market share in market share in excess of 25 per cent. (the 'market share' test). Secondly, where the gross value of the assets of the acquired enterprise (not the value of the assets actually taken over) which ceases to be distinct exceeds £30 million (the 'size of assets' test).

If the OFT considers that there are sufficient reasons for seeking an investigation, the Director General of Fair Trading (DGFT) will advise the Secretary of State of that fact. The Secretary of State may then exercise his discretion to refer the merger to the MMC. If referred, the MMC will advise the Secretary of State of the conclusions of its investigation and, in particular, whether the merger operates, or may be expected to operate, against the public interest. If the MMC concludes that the merger is unlikely to be detrimental to the public interest, the Secretary of State cannot block the merger. However, if the public interest is likely to be prejudiced, he may, in his discretion, block the merger or, alternatively, allow it to proceed.

2   VOLUNTARY PRE-NOTIFICATION PROCEDURE

The Act has introduced a new voluntary pre-notification procedure, to provide a means by which the acquirer may gain clearance for the proposed merger in advance. The acquirer must submit certain information to the OFT and comply with certain conditions. If this is done, the bidder receives automatic clearance, unless the OFT indicates to the contrary, within twenty working days.

The pre-notification system is designed to facilitate the process of examining and clearing mergers quickly, especially where it is clear at an early stage that a reference would not be justified, as in the majority of cases.

At present, there is no requirement for a company to inform the DGFT before merging with another company. However, many companies have chosen to do so, finding it advantageous to discuss (in confidence, if necessary) the proposals in advance. The OFT has also found this useful.

As the new pre-notification procedure is not mandatory, there remains no obligation upon merging enterprises to discuss the proposed merger with the OFT. However, the new provisions do introduce some certainty into the process of examining mergers and are likely to encourage companies to approach the OFT on announcement of the merger.

It should be stressed that the pre-notification procedure does not permit companies to approach the OFT in secret, apply for clearance and merge after twenty working days, safe in the knowledge that the merger will not then be referred. Instead, the proposed merger must have been made public and a statement to that effect included in the merger notice (see 2.1 below). A failure to include such a statement, or the giving of a false statement in the notice, will enable the DGFT to reject the merger notice. Clearance cannot then be given.

The effect of the new provisions is to restrict the power of the Secretary of State to make a merger reference where prior notice has been given to the OFT. The details are discussed below.

2.1 Submission of 'merger notice'

The acquirer (or bidder) may give notice, a 'merger notice', to the DGFT of any proposed arrangements which might result in the creation of a merger situation qualifying for investigation. The notice must be in a form prescribed by the DGFT and state that the proposals it contains have been made public. *S146 SS75A(1) &(2), 75E FTA73*

Once he receives the merger notice, the DGFT has to consider whether the proposed arrangements are likely to prejudice competition so as to create a merger situation qualifying for investigation. He must also take such action as he considers appropriate to bring: *S146 S75B(1) FTA73*

(a)   the existence of the proposal;

(b)   the fact that a merger notice has been given; and

(c)   the date on which the period for considering the notice is to expire

to the attention of all persons who, in his opinion, are likely to be affected if the arrangements are carried into effect.

Where the period for considering the notice expires without the Secretary of State making any reference to the MMC, the arrangements cannot then form the basis of a reference in the future, unless they fall into one of the following exceptions: *S146 SS75A(3) &S75C (1)(a)-(g) FTA73*

(a)   where the merger has still not taken place six months after the end of the period for considering the merger notice;

(b)   where, before the end of the period, the enterprises merge with each other, or with some other enterprise previously unconnected with the proposed merger; and

(c)   where any information which is material to the notified arrangements is not disclosed to the Secretary of State or the DGFT or, if it is disclosed, where it is false or misleading in a material respect.

The period for considering a notice is twenty working days beginning with the day after the DGFT receives the notice and any fee payable to the DGFT has been paid. If the DGFT is unable to complete his enquiries within this period, he may extend the period for a further ten days. If the period is to be extended, the DGFT must give notice of that fact to the person who supplied the merger notice, before the original period for considering the notice has expired. The Secretary of State, however, can require the DGFT to extend the period. This may occur, for example, where he is still considering the DGFT's advice before deciding whether to refer the merger. There are also provisions for further extension of the period. *S146 S75B(2), (3),(6) &(9) FTA73*

During the period for considering the notice, the DGFT may request the person who gave the merger notice to provide further information by a specified date.

S146
S75B(4)
FTA73

2.2   Rejection of merger notice

Within the period for considering the merger notice, the DGFT may reject it if:

S146
S75B(7)
FTA73

(a)   he suspects any of the information supplied by the person giving the merger notice to be false or misleading in a material respect;

(b)   he suspects that the proposed arrangements are unlikely to be carried into effect; or

(c)   any prescribed information is not given in the merger notice, or the information requested by the DGFT from the person who gave the merger notice is not provided within the specified period.

2.3   Power to make regulations

The Act gives the Secretary of State power to make regulations to supplement the provisions outlined above. It is likely that they will deal with the manner in which information may be provided or disclosed to the DGFT and the way in which a merger notice is to be given, rejected or withdrawn.

S146
S75D
(1)&(2)
FTA73

The Secretary of State can also amend the new provisions by regulations for the purpose of determining the effect of giving a merger notice and the steps to be taken by any person in connection with such a notice.

S146
S75F(1)
FTA73

3   UNDERTAKINGS AS ALTERNATIVE TO A MERGER REFERENCE

The Act has amended the FTA73 so as to enable a merger reference to be avoided. This can be done by the Secretary of State accepting undertakings to divest part of a merged business.

Previously, the Secretary of State could ask the DGFT to seek statutory undertakings from the parties concerned with the merger, but this could be done only after the MMC had concluded that the merger in its proposed form, would have operated, or could have been expected to operate, against the public interest.

S88
FTA73

Statutory undertakings, for example, may require the disposal of all or part of existing shareholdings, or interests in shares, in the target company; or require the exercise of voting powers in respect of shares in the target company to be limited. If a party fails to fulfil an undertaking that it has given, the Secretary of State may make an order to remedy or prevent any adverse effect on the public interest.

It is quite common for parties engaged in merger activity to discuss their proposals with the OFT to gauge the reaction of the authorities to the proposed merger. Should the reaction be that there may be an adverse effect on competition, parties have on occasions attempted to give undertakings to divest parts of their business, or parts of the merged business, in order to avoid the occurrence of a monopoly situation and, therefore, a merger reference being made. This practice, commonly known as 'plea bargaining', lacks certainty and has caused a number of problems. In particular, undertakings given by a party to a proposed merger amount to little more than a 'gentleman's agreement' and are not legally enforceable. Therefore, where a party has given an undertaking and failed to abide by it after the merger has gone through, the authorities are, by then, powerless to refer the merger. The new provisions essentially extend the existing process to enable enforcement of undertakings.

However, one apparent deficiency in the new provisions might be in relation to a hostile bid, where the acquiring enterprise submits proposals to the OFT. It is possible that the target enterprise might be prejudiced by the fact that the acquiring company had engaged in plea bargaining with the OFT behind closed doors, in an effort to alleviate those factors which might cause the proposals to give rise to a merger situation qualifying for investigation. Although regulations may provide details of who is able to submit a merger notice, at this stage it is unclear whether they will provide for the other enterprises concerned with the proposals to be made party to, or be involved in, the plea bargaining process.

The new provisions are discussed below.

3.1 Acceptance of undertakings

The Secretary of State may accept undertakings where the DGFT has advised him that in his opinion a referral should be made because the proposed merger is likely to adversely affect the public interest. *S147 S75G(1) FTA73*

In these circumstances, the Secretary of State may accept such undertakings as he thinks appropriate in order to remedy or prevent the adverse effects on the public interest, as specified in the advice of the DGFT. The Act does not give any guidance as to what the Secretary of State might consider to be 'appropriate' in these circumstances. Nevertheless, the undertakings must provide for a divestment in the form of a division of a business, the division of a group of interconnected bodies corporate, or the separation of enterprises which are under common control. *S147 S75G(1) &(2) FTA73*

If the Secretary of State accepts one or more undertakings, he is then prevented from making a merger reference to the MMC unless he has not been notified of all the material facts. *S147 S75G(4) &(5) FTA73*

3.2   Publication of undertakings

The Secretary of State will publish details of the undertakings, together with the
advice given to him by the DGFT in respect of potential adverse effects on the
public interest, and any variation or release of such an undertaking. However, he
will exclude from publication any matters contained in the DGFT's advice which
relate to the:

S147
S75H(1),
(3) & (4)
FTA73

(a)   private affairs of an individual; or

(b)   affairs of a particular body of persons, whether corporate or otherwise

if, in his opinion or that of the DGFT, publication might be prejudicial to the
interests of such persons, unless publication would be in the public interest or is
necessary for the purposes of the advice.

The publication of undertakings is necessary so that third parties are made aware of
the position with regard to the merger. This is particularly so in view of their
ability to bring proceedings in the event of a breach (see 3.4 below). For the same
reason, publication of any variation or release of the undertaking is needed.

The Act confers absolute privilege on any advice given by the DGFT by virtue of
these provisions. As a result, any person who feels that certain statements
contained in the advice are defamatory to him is prevented from taking legal action.

S147
S75H(5)
FTA73

3.3   Keeping undertakings under review

Once the Secretary of State has accepted an undertaking, the DGFT must review
how it is carried out. Where circumstances have changed and the undertaking is no
longer appropriate, he can release one or more of the parties, vary the undertaking,
or provide for it to be superseded by a new undertaking.

S147
S75J(a)
FTA73

3.4   Where undertaking is not fulfilled

Where an undertaking has been accepted, any person may bring civil proceedings
in respect of a failure by the person giving the undertaking to fulfil its terms.

S148
S93A
FTA73

Where it appears to the Secretary of State that an undertaking accepted by him is
unlikely to be fulfilled, he may make an order by statutory instrument to remedy or
prevent the adverse effects specified in the advice given by the DGFT. Such an
order may even declare the merger in its present form to be unlawful. The
Secretary of State must in any event take account of the advice given by the DGFT
when determining whether, or to what extent, or in what manner, he may exercise
this power. Civil proceedings may lie in the event of a failure to comply with the
provisions of the order.

S147
S75K
(1)-(3)
FTA73

The order may contain provisions that are different to those appearing in the
undertaking. Once the order is made, the undertaking no longer applies.

S147
S75K(4)
&(5)
FTA73

4   TEMPORARY RESTRICTIONS ON SHARE DEALINGS

For many years, there has been an understanding in business circles that no party subject to a merger reference would acquire shares in the target from the moment the reference was announced. The Act has now made this law. In particular, new provisions have been introduced which prohibit parties to a merger from acquiring each other's shares, except with the consent of the Secretary of State, from the time the merger is referred to the MMC. The prohibition is designed to prevent the building up of holdings which might prejudice the outcome of the MMC investigation. Parties to a merger will remain subject to this prohibition from the moment that the prospective merger is referred and for the duration of the MMC investigation.

This change has been introduced because of the action taken by Elders IXL Limited in 1988 in the course of their subsequently unsuccessful bid for Scottish & Newcastle Breweries plc. In that case, Elders acquired shares in Scottish & Newcastle immediately upon the announcement of the referral and prompted the Secretary of State to make an order restricting further acquisitions. The new provisions will, therefore, make it unnecessary for the Secretary of State to make such an order in those circumstances. The new provisions are discussed below.

4.1   The restriction

The Act makes it unlawful, except with the consent of the Secretary of State, for any person who is a party to a merger which has been referred to the MMC to acquire shares in any other such person. *S149 S75(4A), (4F)& (4G) FTA73*

This prohibition operates from the announcement by the Secretary of State of the making of the merger reference until : *S149 S75(4B) [FTA73*

(a)   the reference is laid aside or when the time granted to the MMC for making its report on the reference expires: or

(b)   the MMC's report is laid before Parliament (except when the report contains conclusions highlighting adverse effects on the public interest, in which case the period ends forty days after the report is laid before Parliament).

Nevertheless the acquisition of an interest in shares may be lawful if the Secretary of State gives his consent to it. Such consent may be a general consent to purchase an interest in shares, or it may be more specific, such as allowing acquisitions only up to a certain level. The Secretary of State has the power to revoke any consent that he may give. The Secretary of State must publish, if necessary, any consent given so as to ensure that all of the parties involved are aware of it . *S149 S75(4A) &(4C) (a)-(b) FTA73*

Where a party to a merger acts in contravention of these provisions, the Secretary of State may institute civil proceedings with a view to obtaining an injunction or other appropriate relief. *S149 S75(4D) FTA73*

5   OBTAINING CONTROL BY STAGES

The merger reference powers in the FTA73 recognise three degrees of control which can create a merger. These are the ability to exercise influence over the other entity, to control policy, and the acquisition of a controlling interest. Each one can give rise to a merger situation qualifying for investigation. However, these provisions have proved unable to deal with situations where control of a company was obtained in stages as any acquisition of shares which occurred more than six months previously could not be taken into account unless new material information emerged. Therefore, the MMC was in a position where it could not look at previous acquisitions which no longer qualified for investigation; on the other hand, if a reference was made too early, it might decide that there was no merger to examine.

The Act provides that where an enterprise is brought under the control of a person or a group of persons in the course of two or more transactions (i.e. a 'series of transactions') then, for the purposes of the merger reference, they may be treated as having occurred simultaneously on the date on which the last of them occurred. *S150 S66A(1) FTA73*

Only a series of transactions which occur within a two year period may be treated as having occurred simultaneously. In determining the time at which any transaction occurs, no account is taken of any option or other conditional right until that option is exercised or the condition is satisfied. *S150 S66A(4), (6) FTA73*

Where a series of transactions includes a transaction in which a controlling interest is obtained in the enterprise, any subsequent transaction is disregarded for the purposes of the merger reference. The existing provisions of the FTA73 apply for the purposes of determining whether an enterprise is brought under the control of a person, or group of persons, or whether the enterprise is brought under common control. *S150 S66A(3) &(5) FTA73 SS65&77 FTA73*

The advantage of these new provisions is that it will no longer be possible to argue that the merger had occurred at an earlier date, by virtue of an earlier transaction, and that it is now too late for the authorities to intervene. Instead, the Secretary of State or, as the case may be, the MMC may treat the date of the last transaction as the point at which the period for referring the merger begins.

6   FALSE OR MISLEADING INFORMATION

It will be an offence for a person to furnish information (either directly or through someone else) to the Secretary of State, the DGFT or the MMC in relation to mergers and other competition matters if he knows, or is reckless as to whether, the information is false or misleading in a material particular. *S151 S93B(1) FTA73*

7 FEES

The Act gives the Secretary of State power to make regulations to require the payment to him, or the DGFT, of fees in connection with the exercise of their functions, or those of the MMC, under Part V (Mergers) of the FTA73. S152(1)& (2)

The fact that companies who wish to have their mergers cleared might have to pay towards the expenses incurred by the authorities in giving the necessary clearance has not been welcomed by many sections of industry. Nevertheless, the provisions are consistent with those sections appearing in the Act which endeavour to recover fees in relation to DTI investigations (see Chapter 7 at 4.6).

Chapter 7

Investigations

1   SUMMARY

In May 1988, the Government concluded its review of investigation powers and procedures by announcing certain measures intended to improve the system of investigations.   The Act has implemented these measures by amending and extending the existing statutory provisions relating to investigations and the power to obtain information under the following legislation:

*   Companies Act 1985 (the 1985 Act);

*   Company Directors Disqualification Act 1986 (CDDA86);

*   Financial Services Act 1986 (FSA86);

*   Insolvency Act 1986 (IA86); and

*   Insurance Companies Act 1982 (ICA82),

thereby strengthening the Secretary of State's powers of investigation.

The changes introduced by the Act work in two ways. Firstly, they simplify but, at the same time, enhance the existing powers to obtain and disclose information. These changes, which create greater consistency between the various pieces of legislation, are intended to speed up investigations and make the process more effective while simultaneously safeguarding the proper interests of those persons involved.

Secondly, they set up a new regime which confers certain powers on the Secretary of State to assist overseas regulators. As a result of the growing internationalisation of the securities industry, cooperation between international authorities has increased in recent years. With financial markets becoming more internationalised, so too has the capacity for corporate wrongdoing. In an effort to combat such abuses, the Act has conferred upon the Secretary of State certain new powers which he may exercise on receipt of a request for assistance from an overseas regulatory authority.

The Government hopes that these changes will maintain the fairness and efficiency of markets, which is the main purpose of the investigation powers.

2   POWERS TO OBTAIN INFORMATION

2.1   Inspectors' powers extended to 'the matter', not the company

Under the 1985 Act, documents and evidence required to be produced had to relate 'to the company'; the Inspectors had the power to obtain this from officers and agents of the company and from 'any other person'. This power has been extended and the Act now provides that the information must relate to 'a matter which they (the inspectors) believe to be relevant to the investigation'. *S56(3)* *S434(2)*

As a result of this, inspectors can obtain information from any person so long as it relates to a matter which they believe to be relevant to the investigation. This clearly enhances their power to obtain information. In addition, the subjective approach taken by the Act (i.e. '..which they believe to be relevant..') means that the inspectors do not have to demonstrate that the information requested relates to the company or is actually relevant.

2.2   Books, papers and records defined as 'documents'

The Act defines 'documents' to include information recorded in any form. Various references to books, papers and documents in the 1985 Act should be substituted with references to 'documents'. *SS56(5), 63(7), 66(4)* *SS434(6) 447(9), 450(5)*

For the purposes of the ICA82, 'documents' is substituted for 'books or papers' and includes information recorded in any form. *S77(2)* *S44(6)* *ICA82*

These changes result in consistency between the 1985 Act and related provisions in the ICA82 and the FSA86.

2.3   New power to issue warrant when documents may be interfered with

To supplement the existing powers of entry and search of premises, the Act has made the following changes.

2.3.1   *Companies Act 1985*

Inspectors may now obtain a warrant to enter premises and search for documents that they had not previously asked for. Under the 1985 Act, a warrant could only be obtained when documents had not been produced as required. To obtain the *S64(1)* *S448(2)* warrant, however, the inspectors must have reason to believe that a serious offence (one which carries a penalty in excess of two years' imprisonment) has been committed. They must also believe that there is a danger that the relevant documents may be removed, tampered with or destroyed unless the element of surprise is available.

An inspector may now also take copies of any documents relating to the offence. Furthermore, he can require any person named in the warrant to provide an explanation of them or to state where they may be found.

S64(1)
S448(3)

In addition, a warrant obtained under S448(2) may also authorise the inspectors to take possession of, or copies of, other documents that they believe are relevant to the investigation.

S64(1)
S448(4)

Obstruction of an inspector will only be an offence if it was done intentionally. This change increases the protection of persons who are being investigated.

S64(1)
S448(7)

2.3.2   Financial Services Act 1986

The Act has removed a restriction so that a person to whom a warrant has been issued may require the production of documents from any premises specified in the warrant, irrespective of the identity of the owner or occupier. The FSA86 only allowed the production of documents from premises that were owned or occupied by a person whose affairs were being investigated.

S76(2)
S199
(1) & (2)
FSA86

2.3.3   Insurance Companies Act 1982

The Act has also introduced similar provisions to those in 2.3.1 above into the ICA82.

S77(3)
S44A
ICA82

2.4   Widening of Secretary of State's powers to delegate

The Secretary of State may now authorise 'any other competent person' to exercise his power to require the production of documents. A competent person (likely to be a lawyer or an accountant) who is appointed, will be required to report to the Secretary of State. Under the 1985 Act, the Secretary of State could only delegate these powers to his officers; this introduces a power consistent with that available to him under the FSA86.

S63(4)
S447(3)

2.5   Amendments to the protection of banking information

2.5.1   Companies Act 1985

The Act gives three exceptions to the general rule that a person cannot be required to disclose information or produce documents in respect of which he owes an obligation of confidence by virtue of carrying on banking business. These are:

S69(3)
S452(1A)
&(1B)

(a)   if the person to whom the obligation is owed is the company or other body corporate under investigation;

(b)   if the person to whom the obligation of confidence is owed consents to the disclosure or production;or

(c)   if the requirement to disclose is authorised by the Secretary of State.

The first two exceptions are unlikely to cause much concern. However, the same may not be said of the third, which provides the Secretary of State with the ultimate power to require disclosure regardless of confidentiality issues. The Government has recognised that confidentiality is important but, nevertheless, takes the view that the investigation is equally important. In any event, it is envisaged that the Secretary of State will want to be satisfied that the information can properly be so required, and further that the information is relevant to the investigation.

It should be noted that the general rule referred to above does not apply where the person owing the obligation of confidentiality is the company or other body corporate under investigation.

Under the 1985 Act, the extent of the privilege against disclosure of confidential information was a little unclear. The Act has therefore sought to clarify the matter.

2.5.2   *Financial Services Act 1986*

Similar provisions to those discussed in 2.5.1 above have been introduced into the FSA86, clarifying the powers of officers and other competent persons to demand the disclosure of information in the investigation of collective investment schemes (unit trusts), investigations into insider dealing and investigations into persons carrying on investment business.

SS72(2), S73(5) 74(4) SS94(7) 105(2A) &177(8) FSA86

3   DISCLOSURE OF INFORMATION

3.1   To other competent authorities

The Act makes a number of minor changes to the existing legislation regarding the disclosure of information to other competent authorities. These changes are in keeping with the overall aim of the Act; in particular, they ensure harmonisation of related legislation and clarify the extent of powers of investigation and the proper use of information obtained.

Under the 1985 Act, provisions existed to provide security for information obtained in the course of investigations. To this end, the 1985 Act defines the circumstances in which the information may be disclosed; in the main this is to enable or assist other investigations or criminal proceedings. Information obtained can be disclosed to certain specified bodies; officers or servants of these bodies have been added to the list.

S65(6) S449(3)

There are three significant additions to the list of circumstances in which information may be disclosed. These are:

(a) in relation to any disciplinary proceedings relating to the discharge by a public servant of his duties;

S65(2)(h)
S449(1)
(ll)&
(1A)(a))

(b) for the purpose of enabling or assisting an overseas regulatory authority to exercise its regulatory functions (see 6 below); and

S65(2)(i)
S449
(1)(m)

(c) for the purpose of enabling or assisting a RSB or RQB (see Chapter 5 at 2) to exercise its regulatory functions.

S65(2)(g)
S449(1)
(hh)

These changes are also introduced into the FSA86.

S75(3)(c),
(d)&(f)
S180(1)
(hh),(oo),
(qq)
FSA86

3.2   Disclosure by inspectors

Minor changes have been made to the 1985 Act and the FSA86 so that they have consistent provisions enabling inspectors to disclose information to other inspectors, appointed under the relevant sections. Similar rights extend to 'persons authorised to exercise powers', i.e. disclosure may be made to such persons, not by them (see 2.4 above), or officers or servants of such persons, under the 1985 Act, the FSA86, the ICA82 or the Act. Under the 1985 Act, the information could only be disclosed to the Secretary of State.

S68
S451A(3)
(b)&(4)

The Secretary of State has been given some additional powers of disclosure and may, if he thinks fit, disclose any information obtained in relation to the ownership of shares under section 444 (power to obtain information as to those interested in shares) of the 1985 Act, to the following persons:

S68
S451A(5)

(a) the company whose ownership was subject to the investigation;

(b) any member of the company;

(c) any person whose conduct was investigated in the course of the investigation;

(d) the auditors of the company; or

(e) any person whose financial interests appear to the Secretary of State to be affected by matters covered by the investigation.

3.3   Restrictions on disclosure under the FSA86

The list of persons who are restricted from disclosing information obtained in the course of their functions under the FSA86 (primary recipients), has been extended to include anyone named in a warrant issued under the Act.

S75(1)(c)
S179(3)
(j)
FSA86

The list of those to whom such information may be disclosed under the FSA86 has been amended along the lines discussed in 3.1 above.

S75(2)-
(7)
S180
FSA86

4 REPORTS OF INVESTIGATORS

4.1 Investigations by inspectors not leading to published report

The Act allows inspectors to be appointed on the specific terms that any report they make will not be published. The aim of this provision is not to enable a full investigation to be carried out but merely to determine whether grounds exist for a specific prosecution or, alternatively, regulatory action. The decision not to publish the report is made at the outset. Furthermore, the Act prevents the Secretary of State from publishing a report compiled by the inspectors. Under the 1985 Act, inspectors had, at the conclusion of their investigation, to submit a final report to the Secretary of State, which he was entitled to publish. *S55 S432(2A)*

In view of the fact that much of our existing legislation purports to protect the public interest, this change raises an interesting question. If inspectors are appointed on terms that their report will not be published, what is the position if the investigation reveals, and the final report to the Secretary of State contains, material which, in the public interest, ought to be disclosed? Should the Secretary publish the report, even though he does not have the statutory power to do so? Or, should he refuse publication, and thereby ignore an ordinary person's right to know about issues which might affect him? For example, a person who suffers from the stigma of being investigated may be cleared in the final report. However, should the report, which clears his name, not be published, the person investigated will understandably feel aggrieved. The position remains unclear. The Government, however, has indicated that the inspectors could be re-appointed under section 432 (other company investigations) of the 1985 Act, which would enable the results of their enquiries to be published.

4.2 Power of Secretary of State to curtail an investigation

4.2.1 *Transfer to appropriate prosecuting authority*

The Act confers on the Secretary of State a power to curtail an investigation when it becomes clear that a criminal offence may have been committed and the matter has been referred to the appropriate prosecuting authority. *S57 S437(1B)*

From the wording of the new provision it is unclear when the Secretary of State should consult the relevant prosecuting authority. Should it be as soon as there is a suggestion that a criminal offence has been committed? It would appear that the provisions are intended to be used to stop or curtail an investigation, in circumstances where there would be no reason to continue once the matters suggesting a criminal offence have been uncovered.

Where the matter has been transferred to the relevant prosecuting authority, the inspectors need not submit a final report to the Secretary of State unless their appointment was pursuant to an order of the court (this does not apply under the FSA86), or unless the Secretary of State directs otherwise. *S57 S437(1C)*

Subject to the exception mentioned above, identical provisions have been introduced into the FSA86, enabling the Secretary of State to curtail investigations.

S72(3)
S94(8A)
&(8B)
FSA86

4.2.2   Insider dealing

The Secretary of State now has the power to direct the inspectors to take no further steps in an insider dealing investigation under the FSA86, or to take only such steps as are specified in his direction.

S74(3)
S177(5A)
FSA86

This new provision merely enhances the Secretary of State's ability to ensure that the investigation is properly directed so that the possible insider dealing offence can be dealt with quickly.

4.3   All reports now admissible in legal proceedings

A copy of any report compiled by inspectors appointed under Part XIV of the 1985 Act, and certified by the Secretary of State to be a true copy, will be admissible in any legal proceedings as evidence of the opinion of the inspectors in relation to any matter contained in the report.

S61
S441(1)

Previously, such reports were only admissible as evidence of the opinion of the inspectors when they were appointed under section 431 (investigation on application of company or its members) or 432 (other company investigations) of the 1985 Act. This had caused problems. For example, if inspectors were appointed under either section 442 or 446 of the 1985 Act (to investigate company ownership or share dealings respectively), their final report was not admissible as evidence of their opinion in relation to the matters contained in the report. To overcome this problem, a further investigation had to be carried out under section 431 or 432.

Therefore, by making all reports of inspectors appointed under Part XIV of the 1985 Act admissible, there will be no need to follow this slow and inefficient route in order to use such reports as evidence. It should be noted that, in any event, the law of evidence ultimately determines the admissibility of evidence.

4.4   Power to bring civil proceedings on company's behalf

The Secretary of State now has the power to bring civil proceedings on a company's behalf, where it appears from *any* report made or information obtained under Part XIV of the 1985 Act, that it is in the public interest to do so.

S58
S438(1)

Under the 1985 Act, such proceedings could only be commenced on the basis of a report made under section 437 (inspectors' reports), or information or documents obtained under section 447 (Secretary of State's power to require production of documents) or 448 (entry and search of premises).

It is possible for information to be obtained by virtue of provisions other than those of sections 437, 447 and 448. Because of this, and the importance of acknowledging the public interest element, the Act has extended the existing power to cover all information obtained under Part XIV of the 1985 Act.

4.5   Investigation of foreign companies

The Act has clarified the applicability of Part XIV of the 1985 Act to bodies corporate incorporated outside Great Britain which carry on, or have at any time carried on, business in Great Britain. Previously, the 1985 Act specified that investigations could be carried out under certain sections of Part XIV, but this left some uncertainty as to the applicability of other investigative powers. The Act now specifies that Part XIV applies in its entirety, subject to certain exceptions. These are: investigations brought under section 431 (investigation on application of company or its members), section 438 (power to bring civil proceedings on company's behalf), sections 442 to 445 (investigation of company ownership and power to obtain information as to those interested in shares, etc.) and section 446 (investigation of share dealings).

S70
S453(1),
(1A)&
(1B)

4.6   Costs of investigation

4.6.1   *Companies Act 1985*

The applicant is liable for the expenses of an investigation into the ownership of a company on the application of the company's members, to such extent as the Secretary of State may direct. Under the 1985 Act, such a direction by the Secretary of State could only be made where inspectors are appointed under section 431 (investigation of a company on its own application or that of its members).

S59(4)
S439(5)

The Act clarifies that amongst the expenses of, or incidental to, an investigation, which may be recovered, are such sums as are reasonable in respect of general staff costs and overheads (see also 5 below).

S59(2)
S439(1)

4.6.2   *Financial Services Act 1986*

Expenses may now be sought from persons convicted under certain provisions of the FSA86 in connection with prosecutions arising out of investigations into collective investment schemes, into the affairs of persons carrying on investment business or into insider dealing.

SS72(4),
73(4),
74(6)
SS94(10)
105(11),
177(11)
FSA86

5   RIGHT OF MEMBERS TO REQUIRE INVESTIGATION INTO COMPANY OWNERSHIP

A company's members may still apply for an investigation into their company's ownership. However, there are new provisions which enable the Secretary of State, before appointing inspectors, to require the applicant(s) to give security, not normally to exceed £5,000, for payment of the costs of the investigation.

S62
S442(3)
&(3B)

A similar provision exists under the 1985 Act with respect to investigations into the company's affairs under section 431.

The Government had originally intended to withdraw this right; as a compromise the right remains, but the members of a company who avail themselves of it will have to pay for the resulting investigation.

However, if the Secretary of State is of the view that the powers conferred by section 444 of the 1985 Act are sufficient for the purposes of investigating the ownership of the company's shares, he may instead conduct an investigation under that section. This means that inspectors need not be appointed. Instead, if there is reasonable cause to believe that any person has information about present and past interests in the shares in question, he must disclose the information. *S62 S442(3C)*

6 POWERS EXERCISABLE TO ASSIST OVERSEAS REGULATORY AUTHORITIES

In recent years there has been an increase in international corporate transactions and, inevitably, an increase in undesirable practices. In recognition of this, the Government has introduced into the Act a number of sections designed to increase the Secretary of State's power to assist cross-border enquiries.

The Secretary of State can now obtain information and documents from individuals and organisations, or appoint persons to do this on his behalf, when so requested by foreign regulatory authorities. Prior to the Act, this was not possible unless there was a domestic reason for carrying out such enquiries. Inevitably, UK authorities will increasingly seek the cooperation of their overseas counterparts to assist in the investigation of breaches of our domestic laws. It is hoped that, with these new provisions, the UK will be in a position to reciprocate. Provisions have been introduced to protect the confidentiality of information obtained. Nevertheless, it is clear that such information may be disclosed to any person for the purpose of instituting proceedings, as well as where the information has already been made public from another source. Disclosure may also ensue if it is in pursuance of a EC obligation.

6.1 Similar powers to set up investigations if assistance is requested

The Act confers upon the Secretary of State powers to obtain information similar in scope to those that are available for domestic purposes.

6.1.1 The request for assistance

The Secretary of State must receive a request for assistance from an overseas regulatory authority before he is permitted to exercise the powers conferred by the Act. *S82(1)*

An 'overseas regulatory authority' means a body which, outside the UK, exercises any function corresponding to: *S82(2)*

(a)   a function of the Secretary of State (or where applicable any agency, body or authority) under the ICA82, the 1985 Act or the FSA86;

(b)   a function of the Bank of England under the Banking Act 1987;

(c)   any function in connection with the investigation of, or enforcement of rules relating to, conduct of a kind prohibited by the CS(ID)A85; or

(d)   any function to be prescribed by the Secretary of State (by statutory instrument) relating to companies or financial services.

6.1.2   *Power to require information, documents or other assistance*

On receipt of a request for assistance, the Secretary of State may require any person:

(a)   to attend before him and answer questions (on oath if necessary) or otherwise provide information relevant to the enquiries;   S83(2)(a)

(b)   to produce specified documents which appear to be relevant to the enquiries (subject to legal professional privilege); and   S83(2)(b) &(5)

(c)   to give any other assistance in connection with the enquiries that he is reasonably able to give.   S83(2)(c)

For these purposes, as elsewhere, 'documents' includes information recorded in any form. The Secretary of State may take copies or extracts from the documents produced.   S83(4)& (8)

Any statement made by a person in compliance with these provisions may be used in evidence against him. In addition, any information may be used by the Secretary of State to determine whether it is expedient, in the public interest, to seek disqualification of persons who are or were directors of a company.   S83(6) S79 S8 CDDA86

Before exercising these powers, the Secretary of State must take into account certain factors which are discussed below.   S82(4)

The Secretary of State may authorise an officer of his or any other competent person to exercise the above powers on his behalf. Authority can only be granted for the purpose of investigating a specified person or a specified subject-matter already being investigated at the instigation of the overseas regulatory authority.   S84(1)& (2)

6.1.3   *Reciprocity and factors to take into account*

Before exercising his powers, the Secretary of State must take into account certain factors. In particular, he must consider:

(a)   whether corresponding assistance would be given in that country to a UK regulatory authority;   S82(4)(a)

(b)   whether the enquiries relate to the possible breach of a law which has no   S82(4)(b)
      parallel in the UK or involves the assertion of a jurisdiction not recognised
      by the UK;

(c)   the seriousness of the matter, the importance of the information sought and   S82(4)(c)
      whether it could be obtained by any other means; and

(d)   whether it is in the public interest to give such assistance.   S82(4)(d)

It is hoped by the Government that in return for the assistance offered by virtue of
these new provisions, ever improving levels of help will be forthcoming from
foreign regulatory authorities.

It is important to note that the Secretary of State may investigate matters which do   S82(6)
not necessarily constitute an offence in the UK or in any other country. For
example, the Secretary of State might receive a request for assistance from the SEC
in connection with an enquiry involving insider dealing in West Germany. Insider
dealing is not at present an offence in West Germany (it is covered by a code of
practice and will not be against the law until the current draft directive on the
subject is implemented). This will not of itself prevent the Secretary of State from
assisting in an enquiry. The Act requires him to take account, *inter alia*, of possible
breaches of law and any close parallel provisions that may exist in the UK.

The Secretary of State, nevertheless, may decline to assist unless the overseas
regulatory authority undertakes to contribute towards the cost.

If the Secretary of State receives a request from an overseas regulatory authority   S82(5)
which is a banking supervisory body, he must consult the Bank of England before
deciding to exercise his powers.

6.1.4   *Confidentiality*

Any person who owes an obligation of confidentiality by virtue of carrying on   S84(4)
banking business is not required to disclose confidential information or produce
documents unless disclosure is specifically authorised by the Secretary of State, or
the person to whom the duty of confidentiality is owed consents to the disclosure.

The Act does not appear to take account of the way in which an overseas regulatory
authority might treat confidential information. This may raise some questions
about the extent to which confidential information will be passed by the Secretary
of State to the overseas regulatory authority.

During the Committee Stage in the House of Lords, Lord Young (the then
Secretary of State) gave certain assurances as to confidentiality. In particular,
information would be provided for regulatory purposes only. Furthermore,
attached to such information would be provisions limiting disclosures and uses by
the requesting authorities.

It should be noted that a person authorised by the Secretary of State, other than one   S84(5)
of his officers, is required to submit a report to the Secretary of State regarding the
exercise of the powers and the result.

6.2   Use of the information obtained

The Act lays down the purposes for which the information obtained may be used.
These provisions correspond to the rights given to the Secretary of State under
other legislation, for example, the provisions that relate to the use of information in
Companies Act investigations.

The information obtained may be disclosed:

(a)   to any person for the purposes of any criminal proceedings, civil   S87(1)(a)
         proceedings under the FSA86 or certain disciplinary proceedings;   &(2)

(b)   to assist a relevant authority, including the Director General of Fair   S87(1)(b)
         Trading, the Bank of England, an inspector appointed under the 1985 Act,
         a RSB or RQB (see Chapter 5 at 2), the Building Societies Commission or
         the Secretary of State;

(c)   to the Treasury, if it is in the interests of investors or in the public interest;   S87(1)(c)

(d)   if the information is available to the public from other sources;   S87(1)(d)

(e)   in a summary or collection of information such that the identity of any   S87(1)(e)
         person to whom the information relates cannot be ascertained; or

(f)   in pursuance of any EC obligation.   S87(1)(f)

Except in the above circumstances, disclosure is only allowed with the consent of   S86
the person from whom the information was obtained, and, if different, of the
person to whom it relates.

7   AMENDMENT OF THE INSOLVENCY ACT 1986

There are two changes to insolvency legislation:

(a)   section 440 of the 1985 Act, which deals with the Secretary of State's   S60
         powers to present winding-up petitions, has been repealed but re-enacted   S124A
         in the IA86 with the modifications necessitated by new legislation. The   IA86
         relevant provisions of the Criminal Justice Act 1987, the Criminal Justice
         (Scotland) Act 1987 and the Companies Act 1989 have been added to those
         under which the Secretary of State may act on the basis of reports made or
         information obtained under the legislation he may, if he feels that it is
         expedient in the public interest, present a petition for a company to be
         wound up if the court thinks that it is just and equitable; and

(b) there is an amendment in relation to the prosecution of delinquent officers and members of a company. Where a liquidator submits a report to the prosecuting authority, who in turn refers it to the Secretary of State, there is now an obligation to investigate the matter and such other matters relating to the affairs of the company as appear to require investigation. Under the IA86, the Secretary of State was only required to investigate the matter referred to him.

S78
S218(5)
(a)IA86

Chapter 8

Insolvency

1   SUMMARY

The Act makes major changes in the general law of insolvency where the insolvent person ('the insolvent') operates in a financial market. Procedures adopted by the markets for safeguarding the performance of bargains, and to deal with the consequences of default, will take priority over the exercise by licensed insolvency practitioners of their rights, powers and duties under the Insolvency Act 1986 (IA86) or the Bankruptcy (Scotland) Act 1985 (B(S)A85). These provisions are retrospective in the sense that they can in the main be applied by court order to proceedings under those Acts which began after the Bill was published on December 22, 1988.

The other substantial changes made by the Act in the field of insolvency are those affecting the registration of company charges, dealt with above in Chapter 4 at 3. Among the other changes to insolvency law, the most noteworthy is probably the extension in certain circumstances of the period during which a dissolved company can be restored to the register.

2   FINANCIAL MARKETS AND INSOLVENCY

Any insolvency may have a disruptive effect on the market in which the insolvent operates, if it entails the risk of consequential insolvencies among the insolvent's unpaid creditors. Part VII of the Act is based on the idea that this disruptive effect is particularly grave in financial markets. To safeguard the operations of those markets, the bodies controlling them are given the primary responsibility for administering insolvencies of their participants. The market will complete its own internal procedures in relation to the insolvency. This will involve the setting off of balances to arrive at a net figure due to or from each of the insolvent's market debtors or creditors. Only then will any insolvency practitioner appointed to handle the affairs of the insolvent be able to exercise any powers except in relation to matters outside the market.

Furthermore, the Act seeks to safeguard the performance of contracts made in the market by giving a privileged position to certain charges and assets. Charges will be exempt from important provisions of the general insolvency law if they were granted to the body controlling the market for the purpose of securing debts arising in connection with the performance of a contract. Similar exemptions apply to property pledged as cover for margin in relation to 'market contracts'.

2.1   Market contracts

'Market contracts' are contracts connected with a RIE or RCH.   S155(1)

So far as RIEs are concerned, such contracts are of two types. The first is a   S155(2)
contract made by a member of the RIE (or a non-member subject to its default rules; see 2.2 below), and which is subject to the rules of the RIE. The second type is a contract made by the RIE itself to further the provision of clearing services, which is subject to its rules.

So far as RCHs are concerned, a market contract is a contract made by the RCH,   S155(3)
and subject to its rules, in order to provide clearing services to a RIE.

If a person enters into market contracts in more than one capacity, Part VII applies as if each capacity represented a different person; but being party to a contract includes being party as agent. Regulations may modify this.

2.2   Default rules

The gap left by the removal of the insolvency of operators in financial markets from   S156(1)
the normal operation of insolvency law is filled by an extension to the requirements   &(2)
of the FSA86 for the recognition of an investment exchange or clearing house.   Sch21
The requirements now stipulate that there must be default rules to provide for the inability of a member of the exchange or clearing house to meet his obligations under market contracts.

A RIE may in addition designate, with their consent, non-members to whom the   4Sch21
default rules will apply, if their failure would be calculated to disrupt the market.

The application of the default rules of a RIE to a defaulter acting as principal will   2Sch21
result in the netting off of all claims between the defaulter and any other party. The RIE will certify the several net sums due to the defaulter by, or payable by the defaulter to, other parties.

The application of the default rules of a RCH will result in the determination of a   9Sch21
net sum payable by the defaulter to the RCH, or by the RCH to the defaulter, in respect of all contracts. This will be set off against, or aggregated with, any property provided by the defaulter as cover for margin. The RCH will certify the resulting sum.

RIEs or RCHs must report the sums certified to the Secretary of State, and copy that report to the defaulter and any insolvency practitioner in charge of his affairs. There are provisions for advertisement of the issue of the report, and for disclosure of relevant parts to other parties to contracts with the defaulter. S162

If the defaulter is being wound up or is bankrupt, the certified net sums are treated for the purposes of that insolvency as though they had been due or payable at the commencement of the insolvency. Any such sums may thus go to reduce the claim of a creditor of the defaulter by set-off. To the extent that it arises from contracts entered into by that creditor with notice of the insolvency, the benefit which that creditor derives from set-off is recoverable from the creditor by the insolvency practitioner administering the defaulter's affairs. If the creditor is himself insolvent, the sum so recoverable from him ranks immediately ahead of preferential debts (in England and Wales) or (in Scotland) preferred debts. S163

A RCH and a RIE where the defaulter acted as principal, must have arrangements to inform other parties to contracts with a defaulter promptly of the default and of any decision taken under the default rules. Where the defaulter acted as agent, a RIE must ensure that his principals and the other parties to contracts are informed promptly of the default and of the names of the other party. 3&11 Sch21

RIEs and RCHs may delegate the operation of their default rules to another body or person. They must also co-operate with the Secretary of State, any insolvency practitioner in charge of the defaulter's affairs, and any other authority with responsibility connected with the default. 5,6,12 &13 Sch21

The rules of a RCH must preclude the use to meet a shortfall on a client account of margin provided by a defaulter for his own account. The same applies to the rules of a RIE which provides its own clearing arrangements. This is in addition to the effect of rules made under section 55 of the FSA86 (clients money). 7&14 Sch21

RIEs and RCHs may or may not already have default rules complying with the Act. If the Secretary of State believes in any case that the additional requirements specified by the Act are not met, he must give notice to the body concerned within one month of the coming into force of this part of the Act. After six months, he may revoke the recognition or compel compliance. S156 (3)-(5)

A RIE or RCH must give the Secretary of State at least 14 days' notice of any intended alteration of its default rules. The Secretary of State then has 14 days in which to prohibit the alteration or part of it. If the alteration is prohibited, it is ineffective. S157

2.3   Priority over insolvency law

If a defaulter is subject to proceedings under both the default rules of the RIE or RCH and the IA86 or the B(S)A85, then insolvency law operates subject to the proceedings under the default rules. This also applies to insolvency proceedings S158 in relation to others subject to the rules of the RIE or RCH. If default proceedings have been started, and subsequently insolvency proceedings are commenced in relation to other parties as principal to market contracts with the defaulter, those proceedings also operate subject to the default proceedings.

The Secretary of State may, after consultation, direct a RIE or RCH to take, or not to take, action under its default rules; except that he may not direct that no action be taken if insolvency proceedings have been started in relation to the person concerned. If insolvency law proceedings have started and the RIE or RCH does not take action under its default rules, the insolvency practitioner concerned may apply to the Secretary of State, who then notifies the RIE or RCH. The RIE or RCH then has three working days to decide whether or not to take action under its default rules. If no action is taken then insolvency law operates normally. Otherwise the following modifications to insolvency law apply. `SS166& 167`

Insolvency law does not operate to invalidate a market contract, the default rules of a RIE or RCH, or any rules it has for the settlement of market contracts other than under its default rules. Nor can any insolvency office-holder or court exercise powers under insolvency law in a way that interferes with such rules. If the default rules are in operation, only the net sums which the RIE or RCH finally certifies as due or payable rank for any purposes in the insolvency proceedings. `S159`

No market contract may be disclaimed as onerous by the liquidator or trustee in bankruptcy or sequestration of a defaulter who is the subject of default proceedings. Nor may the court exercise its power under insolvency law to rescind such a market contract on the application of another party to it. Contracts made by the RIE or RCH to realise property provided as margin are protected by the same provisions. `S164(1)`

The provisions of insolvency law which render void any disposals of property made after the commencement of winding up or the presentation of a bankruptcy petition do not apply to market contracts. Nor do they apply to the provision of margin in relation to a market contract, or to the realisation or other disposal by a RIE or RCH of property provided as margin. If the other party, with knowledge of the insolvency, entered into a market contract which would under normal insolvency law be void, the insolvency practitioner concerned can recover any benefit which that other party received from the contract, in priority to that other party's preferential (in Scotland, preferred) debts if that other party is himself insolvent. This does not apply where the other party is a RIE or RCH, except where margin has been accepted with knowledge of the insolvency. `S164 (3)-(6)`

Under the normal operation of insolvency law, the court may order the reversal of the effect of certain pre-insolvency transactions. These involve the disposal of assets of the insolvent for no or inadequate consideration (in England and Wales referred to as transactions at an undervalue' and in Scotland as 'gratuitous `S165` alienations'); or transactions a purpose of which is to put a creditor in a better position in an insolvency than he otherwise would be ('preferences' or 'unfair preferences'). The court may not now exercise these powers in relation to market contracts or the provision of margin or dealings by the RIE or RCH with property provided as margin.

Any person who controls assets or documents of a defaulter must assist the RIE or RCH in its default proceedings; except that legal professional privilege (England and Wales) or confidentiality between client and professional legal adviser (Scotland) is preserved. The fees and expenses of an insolvency practitioner who gives such assistance fall on the insolvent estate. If the estate is inadequate, the insolvency practitioner need not give that assistance unless his fees and expenses are underwritten by the RIE or RCH. S160

The liquidator or trustee in bankruptcy or sequestration of a defaulter must pay no dividend or return of capital without making adequate provision for claims likely to arise as a result of the default proceedings. The RIE or RCH can take legal proceedings against the defaulter for the purpose of the default proceedings without being subject to the restrictions which normally apply to proceedings taken against a debtor subject to administration, winding-up or bankruptcy procedure under IA86 or to sequestration under the B(S)A85. S161 (2)&(4)

2.4   Protection of insolvency proceedings

Some protection is afforded to an insolvency practitioner who cannot exercise his normal powers because of default proceedings. If he satisfies the court that a party to a market contract with the defaulter intends to put assets beyond the reach of the insolvency practitioner before the conclusion of the default proceedings, the court may make an order to protect the position. The court may also relieve the insolvency practitioner from the performance of duties affected by the default proceedings. S161 (1)&(3)

2.5   Delegation of functions and FSA86

The Secretary of State may delegate to a designated agency any of his functions in relation to default proceedings except his powers to make orders or regulations. If, on the coming into force of this provision of the Act a designated agency is already exercising all the functions which can be delegated to it under section 114 of the FSA86, then the delegation to it of Part VII functions will be automatic. S168

Various provisions of the FSA86 designed to ensure compliance with its provisions by a RIE or RCH apply to its obligations under Part VII. S169

2.6   Market charges

The Act defines certain charges which are referred to as 'market charges' and gives them protection from the normal operation of insolvency law. This protection holds good even where the Secretary of State has notified the RIE or RCH of insolvency proceedings but no action has been taken under the default rules.

A market charge is a charge in favour of a RIE or RCH which secures debts or liabilities arising in connection with the settlement or the ensuring of the performance of market contracts. It may also be a charge in favour of someone who assumes the responsibility of payment for computer-assisted transfers of securities. S173

Such a charge may be enforced despite the presentation of an administration petition or the making of an administration order. The court may order steps to protect the holder of a prior charge. An administrator cannot require a receiver appointed under a market charge to vacate office. An administrator, and to a lesser extent an administrative receiver or the receiver of a Scottish company, have certain powers to deal with charged property. These powers cannot be exercised in relation to market charges. Dispositions of property resulting in a market charge, or to enforce a market charge, are not void because they were made after the commencement of winding up or the presentation of a bankruptcy petition; but again there is provision for the recovery by the insolvency practitioner of the benefit derived, with knowledge of the insolvency, by a party to a disposition resulting in a market charge. S175

If property subject to an unpaid vendor's lien becomes subject to a market charge, the charge overrides the lien unless the chargee knew of the lien. S179

2.7   Market property

The Act also contains provisions, for the benefit of RIEs and RCHs, to protect property provided as margin in relation to market contracts. As with the provisions relating to market charges, these apply even if the Secretary of State has notified the RIE or RCH of insolvency proceedings but no action has been taken under the default rules.

Property, other than land, provided as margin may be applied for the purpose despite any prior right over it, unless the RIE or RCH was aware of that prior right at the time the property was provided. No subsequent right may be exercised so as to prevent or interfere with the application by the RIE or RCH of the property. If the RIE or RCH disposes of the property in accordance with its rules, the new owner takes it free of those rights. S177

The Secretary of State may make regulations giving a floating market charge priority over subsequent fixed charges. S178

Property, other than land, held by a RIE or a RCH as margin, or subject to a market charge, is exempt from enforcement procedures by unsecured creditors such as execution, diligence or distress, unless the RIE or RCH concerned gives its consent. If consent is given, those enforcement procedures may go ahead even if they would otherwise be prohibited by the IA86 or the B(S)A85. S180

2.8　Rule-making powers

The Secretary of State is given very wide powers to alter the provisions of Part VII of the Act by regulation. He may alter the definition of 'market contracts'; further modify the law of insolvency in relation to market contracts and default procedures; alter the duties of insolvency practitioners to assist RIEs or RCHs and the duties of RIEs and RCHs in relation to information supplied to them; alter the definition of 'market charges'; integrate Part VII with insolvency law and adapt it to overseas investment exchanges and clearing houses; and further modify the law of insolvency in relation to market charges. These regulations are to be made by statutory instrument subject to annulment by either House of Parliament. SS155, 158,160, 173,174, 185&186 2Sch21

2.9　Extension to other bodies

The Secretary of State may also by such regulations extend the provisions of Part VII to give the rights given to RIEs and RCHs to certain overseas exchanges and clearing houses. S170

This is in addition to those overseas investment exchanges and clearing houses which are themselves recognised under section 40(2) of the FSA86. These are included in Part VII and required to have adequate procedures to deal with default. S156 (2)(c) 15Sch21

Regulations may also give charges granted in favour of those overseas bodies the protection given to market charges; and give the same protection to property provided to them as cover for margin as is given to such property provided to UK bodies. SS176& 181

The Secretary of State may also make regulations applying Part VII to contracts on wholesale money markets where settlement arrangements are provided by institutions listed by the Bank of England or by the Bank of England itself. Again, the protection of charges and of property provided as cover for margin may be extended to those institutions. SS171, 172,176, &181

Finally, charges granted in favour of the following may be given similar protection by regulation to that given by Part VII to market charges: S176(2) (c)(d) &(e)

(a)　the Bank of England;

(b)　authorised persons within the meaning of the FSA86; and

(c)　international self-regulating organisations within the meaning of that Act.

2.10　Retrospective effect

Most of the provisions of Part VII which cause default procedures to override insolvency law and protect market charges from normal treatment under insolvency law can be given retrospective effect by court order, provided that the insolvency proceedings concerned were begun on or after December 22, 1988, the date the S182 Sch22

Bill was published. A RIE or RCH, or the beneficiary of a market charge, must apply to the court for such an order within three months of the coming into force of section 182 of the Act. The order cannot apply to assets which the insolvency practitioner concerned has already distributed, and cannot deprive him of his remuneration costs and expenses. The effect of the order is not to apply the provisions of Part VII as enacted as if they had been law on December 22 1988, but to apply the provisions of Schedule 22 which gives the provisions of Part VII as they stood in the Bill introduced into the House of Lords.

2.11   Miscellaneous

The provision of IA86 on co-operation with courts in other parts of the UK or elsewhere (effectively confined to the Commonwealth and the Republic of Ireland) applies to Part VII. There are useful indemnities to protect insolvency practitioners and officers of investment exchanges and clearing houses unless negligence or bad faith is present. SS183 &184

3   OTHER INSOLVENCY IMPLICATIONS

Apart from the provisions of Part VII of the Act relating to financial markets, there are a number of other points where the Act affects insolvency law and practice. Of these, the most important is probably the alteration of the law relating to company charges dealt with in Chapter 4 at 3, since it is when the chargor is insolvent that the chargee seeks to enforce the charge and the registration and validity of the charge are important.

Another change affects the time limit for the restoration to the register of a company which has been wound up and dissolved. There are also various minor amendments to the CDDA86 and to the law of Scotland concerning floating charges.

3.1   Restoration of dissolved company

It is possible for an interested party to obtain a court order restoring a dissolved company to the register. The time within which this can be done is limited to two years in the case of a company which has been duly wound up and then dissolved, and to twenty in the case of a company which has been struck off the register and dissolved without being wound up.

The Act amends this by abolishing the limit even in the case of a company which has been wound up, if the person applying for its restoration is doing so in order to pursue a claim for damages for personal or fatal injuries which is not otherwise obviously time-barred. The amendment is retrospective in that it applies to any company dissolved less than twenty years before the section comes into force, even if it had been wound up and dissolved more than two years before so that the time for restoring it to the register under the 1985 Act had already expired. S141 *S651 (4)-(7)*

Under the Third Parties (Rights against Insurers) Act 1930 claims against an insolvent company of a type in respect of which it carried insurance can be made direct against the insurers. In *Bradley v Eagle Star, 1989 2 WLR 568*, it was decided that this did not help a claimant in respect of an industrial disease where the company had been dissolved and could no longer be restored to the register. The amendment is intended to mitigate the effect of that decision.

The Insolvency Act 1985 contained a provision extending the time limit for a company which has been wound up and dissolved from two to twelve years in any event. That was the only provision of the Insolvency Act 1985 never to have been brought into force and the Act now repeals it. *S212 Sch24*

3.2 Floating charges in Scotland

The Act contains a section making various amendments to the law governing floating charges granted by companies registered in Scotland. The first concerns the date when the floating charge attaches to the property of a company which is wound up by the court. This will now be the date of the winding-up order rather than of the petition on which it was made. *S140*

There are also provisions dealing with the ranking of charges. The rights of the holders of prior charges are confirmed, as is the priority over subsequent charges of a charge which prohibits the creation of prior or equal charges. The maximum amount for which a floating charge to secure a contingent liability can rank in priority to a subsequently registered floating charge is defined.

3.3 Disqualification of directors

Various amendments are made to the Company Directors Disqualification Act 1986 (CDDA86). The most significant of these are:

(a) if the Secretary of State has exercised the powers given to him by the Act to assist an overseas regulatory authority, that investigation may be made the basis of an application for disqualification of a director; and *S79 S8 CDDA86*

(b) section 431 of IA86 (which regulates the conduct of summary proceedings) is now applied to summary proceedings in Scotland against a person who takes part in the management of a company in contravention of a disqualification order or while disqualified as an undischarged bankrupt. *S208 S21(4) CDDA86*

Chapter 9

Financial services

1 SUMMARY

The Financial Services Act 1986 (FSA86) as originally drafted, envisaged that most matters relating to the carrying on of investment business could be dealt with in rules and regulations. However, in practice this has not been the case. Some matters have proved to be of overriding importance and not easily reduced to the type of rules envisaged by the Act. Moreover, the original three-volume set of detailed rules laid down by the Securities and Investment Board (SIB), the body to whom the Secretary of State has delegated the majority of his regulatory powers, has been criticised by many practitioners. In their view, the rules are costly to enforce, and too complex and hard to understand. Concern has also been raised as to potential difficulties that may exist in interpreting the rules. To remedy these problems the Act has introduced three new concepts into the FSA86: statements of principle, designated rules and codes of practice.

Statements of principle are designed to provide a more flexible framework for the formulation of rules which businesses and investors alike will find easier to understand. The designation of rules by the SIB is intended to achieve, where practicable, conformity between the rules of the self-regulating organisations (SROs), while recognising that differences exist in the way members of different SROs carry out investment business. Finally, the introduction of codes of practice will enable certain matters of detail to be dealt with in a more appropriate manner.

The intended effect of these new provisions is to simplify the rules that apply to investment businesses without losing sight of the regulatory objectives. Simpler and clearer rules will make such regulatory objectives easier to understand, thereby enabling practitioners to apply them more effectively. At the same time, some restrictions on the right of action in relation to breaches of the rules have been introduced.

Among the other amendments introduced by the Act are those designed to promote co-operation between regulators internationally and in different parts of the domestic financial sector. Where appropriate arrangements have been negotiated, the SIB or a SRO will be able to rely on other regulators to exercise functions relating to authorisation, monitoring and enforcement.

An important feature of the FSA86 is that most powers of the Secretary of State have been delegated to the SIB. The amendments made by the Act create further powers which it is assumed in this chapter will be delegated to the SIB.

2   SIMPLIFICATION OF RULES

2.1   Statements of principle

2.1.1   *Power to issue statements of principle*

The Secretary of State may issue statements of principle with respect to the conduct and financial standing expected of persons authorised to carry on investment business. Statements of principle will be promulgated by the SIB and apply to all persons authorised under the FSA86 including members of SROs and persons certified by recognised professional bodies (RPBs). It is expected that the SIB will issue broadly expressed statements of principle which will briefly and clearly establish certain fundamental requirements that all authorised persons must satisfy. *[S192 S47A(1) FSA86]*

The conduct expected of authorised persons may include compliance with a code of practice (see 2.3 below) or a standard issued by a body other than the SIB. This enables the SIB to incorporate into statements of principle codes or standards issued by bodies such as The Stock Exchange and the Panel on Take-overs and Mergers. Such codes and standards (e.g. the 'Yellow Book' and the City Code) prescribe good market practice and do not have legal force. *[S192 S47A(2) FSA86]*

Failure to comply with a statement of principle can result in the SIB taking disciplinary action, or exercising its powers of intervention under Chapter VI of Part I of the FSA86. In practice, the relevant SRO or RPB will effect the necessary disciplinary action. Where codes are incorporated, the statement of principle may provide that a failure to comply with the code is a ground for taking disciplinary action or the exercise of powers of intervention. It should be noted that a breach does not of itself give rise to a right of action by an investor or any other person affected. However, where matters covered by statements of principle have legal consequences under the common law, such as actions in negligence or for breach of trust, the right of action is unaffected. Similarly, a breach of a statement of principle will not of itself affect the validity of any transaction. *[S192 S47A(3) &(5) FSA86]*

Rules and regulations made under the FSA86 are usually drafted so as to cover specific circumstances. Not surprisingly, rules drafted in this manner are unlikely to cover every eventuality, particularly matters of general principle. It is important to note that with certain matters being dealt with by statements of principle or in codes of conduct instead of rules, a breach will not necessarily give rise to an action for damages under section 62 of the FSA86 (see 3 below). However, the introduction of statements of principle is likely to assist the effective operation of section 62. Rules are often so complicated that it is not always clear whether or not the rule has in fact been broken. By using statements of principle and codes of practice, guidance for interpreting rules is made available.

2.1.2   *Modification or waiver of statements of principle*

A body responsible for regulating an authorised person may, on the application of that person, modify a statement of principle so as to reflect that person's circumstances or his particular kind of business or even relieve him from the obligation to comply with it. However, the regulatory body must be satisfied that:

S192
S47B
(1)-(3)
FSA86

(a)   compliance with the statement of principle would be unduly burdensome for the applicant having regard to the benefit which compliance would confer on investors; and

(b)   modification or waiver will not result in any undue risk to investors.

The regulatory body can make the modification or waiver subject to conditions.

2.2   Application of designated rules and regulations to members of self regulating organisations

The Secretary of State may designate provisions which will apply to a member of a specific recognised SRO in rules and regulations made under:

S194
S63A(1)
FSA86

(a)   section 48 (conduct of business rules);

(b)   section 49 (financial resources rules);

(c)   section 55 (clients' money regulations); or

(d)   section 56 (regulations as to unsolicited calls).

The designated provisions apply in respect of the carrying on of investment business, in relation to which the member is subject to the rules of the SRO.

Like most of his powers under the FSA86, the Secretary of State's power to designate provisions will be exercised by the SIB. In designating a rule, the SIB may provide that it is to be subject to other rules of the SRO to such an extent as it may specify. As a result, the application of a designated rule may be amplified or qualified by the rules of the SRO.

S194
S63A(2)
FSA86

The effect of designating a rule is that it will apply directly to a member of a SRO as though it were a rule of that SRO and contravention of such a rule will be treated in the same way as a breach of the rules of the SRO.

S194
S63A(3)
FSA86

These new provisions are not intended to generate consistent standards between the SROs. Indeed, SROs are expected to continue to make their own rules within the bounds set by the SIB. However, the SROs must also adopt, as part of their rules, designated rules which are adapted to the circumstances of their members. It should be noted that these provisions do not apply to RPBs.

Similar provisions to those governing the modification and waiver of statements of principle (see 2.1.2 above) apply to the modification and waiver of designated rules. However, the SIB has the power to specify that designated rules may not be modified or waived by a SRO at all or, alternatively, only to such an extent as is specified.

S194(4) SS63A (4)& 63B FSA86

The use of designated rules will reflect the differences that exist between the way investment business is carried on by members of the various SROs. This should generate an improvement in the regulation of SRO members without, it is hoped, affecting the level of protection available to investors.

2.3   Codes of practice

Codes of practice may be issued by the SIB in relation to matters dealt with by statements of principle (see 2.1 above) or by rules and regulations.

S195 S63C(1) FSA86

The provisions of a code of practice issued under these powers are not legally enforceable. Instead, they will assist in determining whether or not an authorised person has complied with a statement of principle or a rule applicable to him.

In relation to statements of principle, a failure to comply with any relevant provision of a code may be relied on as tending to establish a failure to comply with the statement of principle. Conversely, compliance with the code will tend to suggest that the statement of principle was also complied with.

S195 S63C(2) FSA86

Similarly, in relation to matters dealt with by rules and regulations, the contravention of a code of practice does not of itself give rise to liability or invalidate the transaction. Nevertheless, in determining whether or not a person's conduct amounts to a contravention of a rule or regulation, a breach of the code may be relied on as tending to establish liability, whereas compliance may be relied on as tending to negate liability.

S195 S63C(3) FSA86

The SIB may restrict the application of codes of practice where they have the effect of amplifying designated rules so that they conflict with the rules of a SRO.

S195 S63C(4) FSA86

2.4   Standard of protection for investors

The Act has amended the existing criteria which relate to the recognition of SROs and RPBs and which operate to safeguard investors. It does so in two ways.

Firstly, the Act recognises that statements of principle, designated rules and codes of practice as well as rules and regulations made under the Act, are to be taken into account in assessing the level of protection for investors afforded by the arrangements of the SROs and RPBs.

S203(1) &(2) 3(1)Sch2 &3(1)Sch 3FSA86

Secondly, the Act establishes that it is the effect of the SRO's or RPB's rules that is to be taken into account and not their form. At present, the rules of a SRO or RPB which govern the carrying on of investment business by its members or by persons certified by it respectively, must afford investors protection 'at least equivalent to' that afforded by the rules of the SIB. This 'equivalence' test is replaced with a new test which requires the level of protection to be 'adequate'. In this context, regard must be had to:

S203(1) &(2) 3(2)Sch2 &3(2)Sch 3FSA86

(a) the nature of investment business carried on by the members of the SRO or the persons certified by the RPB;

(b) the kinds of investors involved; and

(c) the effectiveness of the arrangements for enforcing compliance.

Therefore, in view of the different kinds of investment business as well as the various types of investor, it is likely that the appropriate level of protection may vary between the various SROs and between the RPBs.

It is envisaged that there will be a transitional period during which these changes are to be phased in. During that time, SROs and RPBs can opt for either the new adequacy test or the equivalence test which it replaces.

S203(3)

2.5 Conclusion

The use of statements of principle, designated rules and codes of practice, should make the rules that apply to investment businesses simpler and easier to understand and apply. It has been suggested by the SIB that this is likely to result in a three tier system of rules. Firstly, statements of principle and codes of practice would prescribe certain required standards that all authorised persons must adhere to. Breach of such principles and codes may result in the authorised person being disciplined by its SRO, although it could not be sued by investors. The second tier would prescribe the main core rules which would be common to all the SROs, and any designated rules issued by the SIB. Private investors could sue an authorised person who contravened such rules. Finally, there would be a more detailed third level comprising the SROs' own rules. The SIB would have to agree that such rules gave 'adequate' protection to investors. A breach of these rules could give a right of action to a private investor.

3 RESTRICTION OF RIGHT TO BRING ACTIONS FOR CONTRAVENTION OF RULES AND REGULATIONS

Where there is a breach of the rules and regulations made under Chapter V of Part I of the FSA86 (conduct of business), an action may only be brought by a 'private investor' who suffers loss as a result of the contravention. The rules and regulations are those made by the SIB and the SROs, including designated rules, as well as the investment business rules of a RPB.

S193(1) S62A(1) FSA86

The meaning of 'private investor' is to be defined by regulations made by the Secretary of State.

S193(1)
S62A(2)
FSA86

As currently drafted, a breach of the above rules and regulations is actionable by any person who has suffered loss as a result of the contravention. The problem with this provision is that it encourages a potentially litigious atmosphere between professional investors. For example, where there is a contravention of the rules, a professional investor may seek to recoup losses incurred, by taking his professional counterpart to court. Due to this problem, the rulebooks have necessarily become more detailed and legalistic in their content and application. Accordingly, the new provision removes the right of practitioners and professional investors to sue for breaches of the rules. As a consequence, room has been made for a simplification of the rulebooks (see 2 above).

S62
FSA86

The Act does, however, provide that the Secretary of State may, by regulation, allow a person, who is not a private investor, to bring such an action in specified circumstances. If rules and regulations are made by a person other than himself, the Secretary of State must, before passing regulations affecting the right to bring an action in respect of a contravention of such rules and regulations, consult that person.

S193(1)
S62A
(1)&(4)
FSA86

It should be noted that where a course of conduct is actionable on other grounds, such as in contract or tort, the ability of non-private investors to bring an action remains unchanged.

Similar new provisions have also been introduced into Schedule 11 to the FSA86 in respect of friendly societies. In particular, the right to sue in respect of a breach of the rules of a recognised SRO for friendly societies, is now restricted to private investors only.

S193(3)
22ASch
11
FSA86

4   COSTS OF COMPLIANCE

The Act has introduced new provisions designed to ensure that the costs imposed on investment businesses by the regulatory process are no more than are necessary to achieve an adequate level of investor protection. In relation to their rules, SROs, RPBs and the SIB must now have satisfactory arrangements for taking into account the cost to their members, or persons certified by them, of complying with such rules.

S204
3ASch 2,
3ASch 3
&2A
Sch 7
FSA86

If a SRO, RPB or designated agency does not have these satisfactory arrangements at the time of commencement of the Act, their status as bodies recognised under the FSA86 is unaffected. However, the Secretary of State may, in such circumstances, give notice to the recognised body within one month of the commencement of the Act pointing out the lack of satisfactory arrangements.

S204(2)
&(5)

Where notice is served on a SRO or a RPB, the Secretary of State cannot revoke the recognition of such a body or apply to the court for a compliance order, until six months after the date on which the notice was served. Similarly, if the order is served on a designated agency, he cannot by order resume all the functions he originally transferred to the agency by delegation order, until six months have elapsed. *S204(3) &(6)*

5   RELATIONS WITH OTHER REGULATORY AUTHORITIES

In the summary in Chapter 7, reference was made to the rapid development of international financial markets and the need to ensure that they operate in a proper and efficient manner. With this in mind, the Act has introduced new provisions intended to improve co-operation between regulatory authorities.

5.1   Reliance on other regulators

Where a member of a SRO or a RPB carries on an activity of a type that is normally regulated by the rules of some other regulatory body, the SIB may take into account the effects of the other body's rules in deciding whether the SRO or RPB satisfies the requirements for recognition. *S196 S128A FSA86*

5.2   Information given and action taken by other regulatory authorities

In relation to a person whose principal place of business is outside Great Britain, or whose principal business is not investment business, the Act has clarified the extent to which the SIB may rely on other appropriate regulatory authorities. Such authorities are those that supervise and control the person in the country where the principal place of business exists or, as the case may be, in relation to his principal business. *S196 S128B(1) FSA86*

Where the SIB is concerned about the activities of a particular person, it may satisfy itself that no action need be taken if the appropriate regulatory authority informs it of that fact; and if it is satisfied as to the nature and scope of the supervision and control exercised by that authority. It is important to note that the SIB retains the responsibility to take action if it knows that something is wrong. *S196 S128B(2) &(3) FSA86*

5.3   Assisting overseas regulators

The Act recognises the need for reciprocity in dealings with overseas regulators. If the SIB is intending to rely on overseas regulators to prevent or restrain misbehaviour overseas, it is to be expected that the opposite should apply and the SIB offer similar assistance if requested. As a result, the SIB may exercise its *S196 S128C FSA86* disciplinary or interventionary powers under the FSA86, at the request of, or for the purpose of assisting, an overseas regulatory authority. In deciding whether to exercise these powers, the SIB may consider, *inter alia*, whether corresponding assistance would be given by that overseas regulatory authority, the seriousness of the case and whether it is in the public interest to give such assistance.

6   DIRECTIONS TO SECURE COMPLIANCE WITH INTERNATIONAL OBLIGATIONS

The only substantive change to the existing provisions has been the addition of recognised investment exchanges (RIEs) and recognised clearing houses (RCHs) to the list of authorities and bodies to whom the Secretary of State may make a direction requiring compliance with certain international obligations. These additions are a consequence of Part VII of the Act (Financial markets and insolvency) which gives certain new functions to RIEs and RCHs (see Chapter 8). These functions might, in certain circumstances, have implications for the carrying out of international obligations. It should be noted that overseas investment exchanges and clearing houses are not included in the list.

S201
S192(2)
(b)&(c)
FSA86

7   OTHER AMENDMENTS

7.1   Amendments in relation to securities

7.1.1   *Offers of securities by private companies and old public companies*

Subject to the Secretary of State granting certain exemptions, a private company, or an old public company (i.e. a company which did not re-register as a public company following the change in definition in 1980), cannot issue, or cause to be issued in the UK, any advertisement offering the issue of its own securities. The circumstances in which the Secretary of State may by order exempt such advertisements have been extended to include any classes of advertisements that he thinks fit.

S199
S170(2)
FSA86

Furthermore, he may now grant an exemption where the securities advertised appear to him to be of a kind that are expected normally to be bought or dealt in only by persons with the necessary expertise and who understand the risks involved.

S199
S170(3)
FSA86

7.1.2   *Offers of short dated debentures*

The Act has amended the circumstances in which certain offers of debentures are not to be treated as offers to the public. The provisions under the FSA86 currently applying to debentures which, under the terms of issue must be repaid within one year of the date of issue, instead now apply to debentures which must be repaid within five years.

S202
S195
FSA86

7.2   Jurisdiction of High Court and Court of Session

With one exception, the Act has essentially redrafted the existing provisions concerning actions brought in the High Court or the Court of Session involving a designated agency, transferee body or competent authority. It is now clear that proceedings may be brought against a recognised SRO in any part of the UK, regardless of whether it has a presence there.

S200
S188
FSA86

7.3   Requirements for recognition of investment exchange

The Act has made it clear that the requirements for recognition of an investment exchange apply to an exchange only insofar as it provides facilities for the carrying on of investment business. An exchange is not required to limit dealings on the exchange to those involving investments.

S205(1)
6Sch4
FSA86

Table of derivations

Set out below is a table which shows the sources, where appropriate, of the sections in the Act. This shows which provisions have been amended and whether the amendments are substantive. The list of substantive changes is cross-referenced to the relevant chapters.

In the table, new section references come in two parts. As elsewhere in this book, the first, in plain text, is the section number in the Act. The second, in italics, is the section as it has been amended or introduced into the appropriate legislation. See Chapter 1 at 5.

New Section	Old Section	Subject	Extent of change
Part 1			
S1		Introduction.	
S2 *S221*	S221	Duty to keep accounting records.	Duties of parent undertakings added; otherwise minor wording changes only. *Ch 3 at 3.5.*
S2 *S222*	S222	Where and for how long records to be kept.	Minor wording changes only.
S3 *S223*	S227(2)	A company's financial year.	Duties of parent undertakings added; otherwise minor wording changes only. *Ch 3 at .3.4.*
S3 *S224*	S224(1)-(3)	Accounting reference periods and accounting reference date.	1. Nine months allowed from incorporation to notify registrar; formerly six months. 2. Default is the last day of the month in which anniversary of incorporation falls; formerly March 31. *Ch 2 at 4.*
S3 *S225*	SS225, 226	Alteration of accounting reference date.	Minor wording changes only, to take account of new definitions. *Ch 2 at 4*
S4(1) *S226*	SS227, 228	Duty to prepare individual company accounts.	Redrafted but effect unchanged.
S4(2)&Sch1		Introduces amendments to Sch4 to the 1985 Act via Sch1.	Largely unchanged. *Ch 2 at 2.6, 2.7 and 10.1; Ch 3 at 3.5.2.*

New Section	Old Section	Subject	Extent of change
S5(1) S227	SS229(1), (5)-(7),230	Duty to prepare group accounts.	Consolidated group accounts to comply with basis of preparation and disclosure per Sch4A. *Ch 3 at 3.*
S5(2)&Sch2		Introduces new Sch4A - form and content of group accounts - via Sch2.	1. Formalises existing practice. 2. Introduces new disclosure requirements. *Ch 3 at 2.5, 3.2.3, 3.4, 3.5.1, 3.5.3-3.5.8, 4.1, 4.1.1-4.1.5.*
S5(3) S228	S229(2)	Exemption for parent companies included in accounts of larger group.	Permits groups to prepare group accounts only for the top EC holding company. Replaces exemption for wholly owned subsidiaries of British companies. *Ch 3 at 3.1.2.*
S5(3) S229	S229(3),(4)	Subsidiary undertakings included in the consolidation.	Circumstances under which subsidiaries may be excluded revised. *Ch 3 at 3.2.*
S5(4) S230	S228(7)	Treatment of individual profit and loss account where group accounts prepared.	New requirement: board approval needed. *Ch 3 at 3.3.*
S6&Sch3 S231&Sch5	S231 except for (2)(d),(e), Sch4, Sch5	Disclosure required in notes to accounts: related undertakings.	Some new disclosure requirements regarding parent companies, joint ventures, associated undertakings, subs excluded, merger relief. *Ch 3 at 4.2 passim.*
S6(3)&Sch4 S232&Sch6	SS231(2)(d), (e), 232, 233	Disclosure required in notes to accounts: emoluments and other benefits of directors and others.	'Golden hellos' now disclosable. Some loopholes in directors' emoluments disclosure closed. Emoluments of employees earning over £30,000 no longer disclosable. *Ch 2 at 2.1 and 2.2.*
S7 S233	S238	Approval and signing of accounts.	Only one director's signature required; previously two. *Ch 2 at 5.3.2(a)*
S8(1) S234	S235	Duty to prepare directors' report.	Minor wording changes only to take account of new definitions. *Ch 2 at 6.*
S8(1) S234A		Approval and signing of directors' report.	New requirement. *Ch 2 at 5.3.1.*
S8(2)&Sch5		Introduces amendments to Sch7 to the 1985 Act via Sch5.	Some new disclosures. *Ch 2 at 6(b).*
S9 S235	SS236,237(6)	Auditors' report.	Minor wording changes only.
S9 S236		Signature of auditors' report.	New requirement. *Ch 2 at 5.3.3*
S9 S237	S237(1),(2), (4),(5)	Duties of auditors.	Minor wording changes only.
S10 S238	S240	Persons entitled to receive copies of accounts and reports.	Redrafted, but effect unchanged.

New Section	Old Section	Subject	Extent of change
S10 *S239*	S246	Right to demand copies of accounts and reports.	Minor wording changes only.
S10 *S240*	SS254,255	Publication of accounts (abridged accounts).	Change in required details from audit report. *Ch2 at 7.*
S11 *S241*	SS241(1),(2), 243(1),(2)	Accounts and reports to be laid before company in general meeting.	Reorganised and redrafted, but effect unchanged.
S11 *S242*	SS241(3), 244	Accounts and reports to be delivered to registrar.	Reorganised and redrafted, but effect unchanged.
S11 *S242A*	S243(3)	Civil penalty for failure to deliver accounts.	Penalties increased. *Ch2 at 5.2.*
S11 *S243*		Accounts of subsidiary undertaking to be appended in certain cases.	New requirement. *Ch 3 at 3.2.3*
S11 *S244*	S242	Period allowed for laying and delivering accounts and reports.	Minor wording changes only, but period allowed may be reduced in future. *Ch 2 at 5.2.*
S12 *SS245, 245A-C*	S245	Provisions in connection with laying or delivering defective accounts.	New provisions. *Ch 2 at 10.2.*
S13(1)&(2)& Sch6 *SS246,247& Sch8*	SS247,248 &249	Qualification of small and medium-sized companies and their exemptions.	1. Persons authorised under the FSA86 may not claim exemption. 2. More details of fixed assets to be given by small companies. *Ch 2 at 8.*
S13(3) *S248*		Exemption for small and medium-sized groups.	New exemption from preparing group accounts. *Ch 3 at 3.1.1.*
S13(3) *S249*		Qualification of group as small or medium-sized.	Similar to existing conditions permitting small and medium-sized groups to file modified accounts but now exempting them from preparing group accounts. Criteria may now be based on the group figures before or after consolidation adjustments with higher limits for the former. *Ch 3 at 3.1.1.*
S14 *S250*	SS252,253	Resolution not to appoint auditors (dormant companies).	Redrafted; authorised persons under the FSA86 cannot be dormant. *Ch 2 at 9.*
S15 *S251*		Provision of summary financial statements to shareholders (listed companies).	New provision. *Ch 2 at 3.*
S16 *S252*		Election to dispense with laying of accounts and reports before general meetings (private companies).	New provision. *Ch 2 at 5.1.*

New Section	Old Section	Subject	Extent of change
S16 S253		Right of shareholders to require laying of accounts (private companies).	New provision. *Ch 2 at 5.1.*
S17 S254	S241(4)	Exemption from requirement to deliver accounts and reports (unlimited companies).	Redrafted but effect unchanged.
S18(1) SS255, 255A-C	SS234,258-262	Special provisions for banking and insurance companies and groups.	1. Special category status for shipping companies has ended. 2. Alternative accounting provisions may only be used if banking or insurance is the predominant group activity. Previously the group only needed to contain a special category company. *Ch 2 at 5.4, 6(c), Ch 3 at 4.3.1.*
S18(2) S255D		Power to apply provisions to banking partnerships.	New power. *Ch 2 at 5.4.2.*
S18(3)&(4)& Sch7		Accounts of banking and insurance companies and groups.	Various minor changes. *Ch 2 at 10.1, Ch 3 at 3.2.3, 4.3.1-4.3.3.*
S18(5)& Sch8		Directors' report where accounts are prepared under Sch9.	More disclosures now required. *Ch 2 at 6.*
S19 S256		Definition of accounting standards.	Accounting standards to be defined by SI. New power to make grants to standard-setting bodies. *Ch 2 at 10.*
S20 S257	S256	Power of Secretary of State to alter accounting requirements.	Wider power. *Ch 2 at 5.2.*
S21& Sch9 S258& Sch10A		Parent and subsidiary undertakings.	Introduces new and wider definition of 'group' for accounting purposes. *Ch 3 at 2.2.*
S22 S259		Meaning of 'undertaking'.	Extends consolidation and other accounting requirements to businesses that are not companies. *Ch 3 at 2.2 and 3.3.*
S22 S260		Participating interests.	Concept of 'participating interest' replaces that of 'related company'. *Ch 3 at 2.5.*
S22 S261		Notes to the accounts may be in a document annexed.	Unchanged provision now in body of Act; previously in Sch. only.
S22 SS262&262A		Minor definitions and index of defined expressions.	Index is new to Act.
S23& Sch10		Consequential amendments.	Various minor amendments. *Ch 2 at 5.2.*

New Section	Old Section	Subject	Extent of change
Part II			
S24		Introduction	
S25	S389(1)-(5)	Eligibility for appointment as auditor.	Membership of RSB a precondition. Bodies corporate now eligible. *Ch 5 at 2.*
S26		Effect of appointment of partnership.	English law clarified; appointment is of partnership, not individual. New rules on succession. *Ch 5 at 3.2.*
S27	S389(6),(7)	Ineligibility on grounds of lack of independence.	New exclusions may be added by SI. *Ch 5 at 3.3.*
S28	S389(9),(10)	Effect of ineligibility.	Minor wording changes only.
S29		Power of Secretary of State to require a second audit.	New power, given in cases where an audit has been conducted by an ineligible auditor. *Ch 5 at 3.4.*
S30&Sch11		Supervisory bodies.	New provisions. *Ch 5 at 2.1, 2.2, 3.1 and 3.3.1.*
S31		Meaning of 'appropriate qualification'.	New requirement. *Ch 5 at 2.3.1.*
S32&Sch12		Qualifying bodies and recognised professional qualifications.	New provisions. *Ch 5 at 2.3.*
S33	S389(1)(b)	Approval of overseas qualifications.	New requirement: additional qualifications to demonstrate sufficient knowledge of UK law and practice may be required. *Ch 5 at 2.3.4.*
S34	S389(1)(b), (2)	Eligibility of persons with 1967 Act authorisation only.	Minor wording changes only.
S35		Register of auditors.	New requirement. Details to be introduced by SI. *Ch 5 at 2.4.*
S36		Information about audit firms to be made available to the public.	As above.
S37-S40		Powers of the Secretary of State to call for information and to enforce compliance with the Act and international obligations.	General powers granted to facilitate efficient operation of Part II of the Act.
S41-S44		Offences.	Offences defined, time limits, jurisdiction, etc.
S45		Fees.	Power to levy fees granted. *Ch 5 at 2.5.*

New Section	Old Section	Subject	Extent of change
S46&Sch13		Delegation of functions of Secretary of State.	Reserve power of Secretary of State to establish a body corporate to which he can delegate any of his functions under Part II of the Act. *Ch 5 at 2.6.*
S47&Sch14		Restrictive practices.	RSB recognition contingent on rule review by DGFT to ensure that restrictions of competition are justifiable. *Ch 5 at 2.2.8.*
S48		Exemption from liability for damages.	Immunity for RSBs. *Ch 5 at 2.2.7.*
S49		Serving of notices.	
S50		Power to make consequential amendments.	
S51		Power to make amendments as a result of changes affecting accountancy bodies.	To enable the Secretary of State to make any necessary changes in the event of the merger etc. of RSBs.
S52		Meaning of 'associate'.	Definition is similar to, but more restricted than, the definition in S346 CA85 of 'connected person'. *Ch 5 at 2.2.2.*
S53		Minor definitions.	
S54		Index of defined expressions.	
Part III			
S55 *S432(2A)*		Investigations without published reports.	New power. *Ch 7 at 4.1.*
S56 *SS434,436*	SS434,436	Production of documents and evidence to inspectors.	1. Widening of powers of inspectors and redrafting of sections. *Ch 7 at 2.1.* 2. Definition of 'document'. *Ch 7 at 2.2.*
S57 *S437(1B), (1C)*		Duty of inspectors to report.	New power to curtail investigations when criminal offences may have been committed. *Ch 7 at 4.2.1.*
S58 *S438(1)*	S438(1)	Power to bring civil proceedings on company's behalf.	Wider powers. *Ch 7 at 4.4.*
S59 *S439*	S439	Expenses of investigating a company's affairs.	1. Clarification of 'expenses'. 2. Liability of applicants in investigations into company ownership. *Ch 7 at 4.6.1.*
S60 *S124A IA86*	S440	Power of Secretary of State to present winding-up petition.	Section repealed in CA, re-enacted with modifications in IA86. *Ch 7 at 7.*
S61 *S441*	S441	Inspectors' reports as evidence.	All reports now admissible as evidence. *Ch 7 at 4.3.*

New Section	Old Section	Subject	Extent of change
S62 *S442(3)-(3C)*	S442(3)	Investigation of company ownership.	New provision: applicants may have to give security for payment of the costs of the investigation. *Ch 7 at 5.*
S63 *S447*	S447	Secretary of State's power to require production of documents.	1. 'Books or papers' redefined as 'documents'. 2. New power to delegate to 'other competent persons'. *Ch 7 at 2.2, 2.4.*
S64 *S448*	S448	Entry and search of premises.	New power to enter premises and search for documents not previously asked for. *Ch 7 at 2.3.1.*
S65 *S449*	S449	Disclosure of information obtained.	Minor changes to the list of 'other competent authorities' to whom information may be disclosed. *Ch 7 at 3.1.*
S66 *S450(4),(5)*	S450(4)	Punishments for destroying company documents.	Minor wording changes only.
S67 *S451*	S451	Punishments for providing false information.	As above.
S68 *S451A*	S451A	Disclosure of information by Secretary of State.	Minor changes enhancing rights of disclosure by inspectors. *Ch 7 at 3.2.*
S69 *S452*	S452	Protection of banking information.	Relaxation of obligation of confidence for banking business. *Ch 7 at 2.5.1.*
S70 *S453(1)*	S453(1)	Investigation of oversea companies.	Increased powers. *Ch 7 at 4.5.*
S71 Sch 22	Sch 22	Investigation of unregistered companies	New provisions on investigations apply to unregistered companies.
SS72,73,74 *SS94,105,* *177FSA86*	SS72,73,74 SS94,105, 177FSA86	Investigations into unit trusts, investment business, insider dealing.	1 Clarification of privilege in connection with banking confidentiality. 2 Power to curtail investigation. 3 Order to bear costs. *Ch 7 at 2.5.2, 4.2.1, 4.2.2 and 4.6.2.*
S75 *SS179(3), 180* *FSA86*	SS179(3),180 FSA86	Restrictions on disclosure of information.	Relaxation of restrictions. *Ch 7 at 3.1 and 3.3.*
S76 *S199FSA86*	S199FSA86	Entry and search of premises.	Extension to powers on issue of warrants. *Ch 7 at 2.3.2.*
S77(2) *S44(6)ICA82*	S44(6)ICA82	Amendments to ICA82.	Redefinition of 'books or papers' as 'documents'. *Ch 7 at 2.2.*
S77(3) *S44A ICA82*		As above.	Similar to changes effected by S64 (S448) above. *Ch 7 at 2.3.3.*
S78 *S218(5)IA86*	S218(5)IA86	Amendment to IA86.	Wider powers. *Ch 7 at 7.*
S79 *S8CDDA86*	S8CDDA86	Amendment to CDDA86.	Investigation for overseas authority a basis of disqualification. *Ch 8 at 3.3.*

New Section	Old Section	Subject	Extent of change
S80 *S53BSA86*	S53BSA86	Amendment to BSA86	Changes consequential on Part III of the Act.
S81 *84(1)BA87*	84(1)BA87	Amendment to BA87	Changes consequential on Part III of the Act.
SS82-91		Request for assistance by overseas regulatory authority.	New legislation. *Ch 7 at 6.*
Part IV			
S92		Introduction	
S93 *S395*		Registration in the companies charges register	Definitions. *Ch 4 at 3.1.*
S93 *S396*	S396	Charges requiring registration	1 Charges created on intellectual property must now be registered. 2 'Registrable charges' may be changed by SI. *Ch 4 at 3.1.*
S94 *S397*	S401	Companies charges register.	The registrar is no longer obliged to issue certificates of registration. *Ch 4 at 3.2.3.*
S95 *S398*	SS399,400, 401,415,416, 417,418	Duty of company to deliver particulars of charge for registration.	The registrar must now send copies of particulars filed and a note evidencing date of filing. *Ch 4 at 3.2.1.*
S95 *S399*	SS395,410	Effect of failure to deliver particulars for registration.	A charge will now also be void as against purchasers of an interest in property subject to a charge. *Ch 4 at 3.2.5(b).*
S95 *S400*	SS404,419	Late delivery of particulars.	New provisions dealing with insolvency proceedings. *Ch 4 at 3.2.5(b).*
S96 *S401*	SS404,419	Delivery of further particulars.	Now possible without a court application. *Ch 4 at 3.2.5(a)*
S97 *S402*	SS395,410	Effect of errors and omissions in particulars delivered.	Reliance on charge is restricted to the rights conferred in the actual particulars filed. In some circumstances the court may order that the charge will not be void against an administrator or liquidator or a purchaser for value. *Ch 4 at 3.2.5(b).*
S98 *S403*	SS403,419	Memorandum of satisfaction or release.	No longer a requirement to submit a statutory declaration. Both company and chargee now required to sign memorandum. New provisions dealing with the delivery of a memorandum where the debt is not satisfied or the charge released. *Ch 4 at 3.2.6.*
S99 *SS404,405, 406&407*		Further provisions with regard to voidness of charges.	Clarification. *Ch 4 at 3.2.8.*

New Section	Old Section	Subject	Extent of change
S100 *SS408-410*	SS397,405, 413	Delivery of particulars.	Additional particulars are to be delivered in respect of debentures of a series, the appointment of a receiver or manager and crystallisation or attachment of floating charges. *Ch 4 at 3.2.7.*
S101 *S411&412*	SS406,407, 408,421,422, 423	Copies of instruments and register to be maintained by company.	English unlimited companies must now maintain a register of charges they create. *Ch 4 at 3.2.2, 3.3.*
S102 *S413*		Supplementary.	
S103 *S414*		Date of creation of a charge.	New provisions. *Ch 4 at 3.2.*
S103 *S415*		Meaning of 'prescribed particulars' and other terms.	
S103 *S416*		Notice of matters disclosed in register.	A person will be deemed to have notice of the matters disclosed in the register at the time the charge is created. *Ch 4 at 3.2.4.*
S103 *S417*		Power of court to dispense with signature.	New powers. *Ch 4 at 3.2.5(a),3.2.6.*
S104 *SS418-420*		Interpretation and defined expressions.	
S105& Sch15	SS409,424	Charges on property of oversea company.	New regime for registration of charges of oversea companies. *Ch 4 at 3.4 passim.*
S106 *Sch22*		Application to unregistered companies.	Legislation amended by this Act will apply to unregistered companies.
S107& Sch16		Consequential amendments.	

Part V

New Section	Old Section	Subject	Extent of change
S108 *S35*	S35	A company's capacity and its objects.	Validity of act of company cannot be called into question by reason of it being beyond powers in memorandum. *Ch 4 at 5.1.*
S108 *S35A*	S35	Power of directors to bind the company.	1. Greater protection for third parties dealing with the company. *Ch 4 at 5.3.* 2. Ability of members to restrain an *ultra vires* act. *Ch 4 at 5.6*
S108 *S35B*	S35(2)	Enquiring as to capacity of company or authority of directors.	No duty to enquire. *Ch 4 at 5.5.*
S109 *S322A*		Invalidity of certain transactions involving directors.	New provisions where director(s) are party to a transaction in which authority of directors has been exceeded. *Ch 4 at 5.4.*

New Section	Old Section	Subject	Extent of change
S110 S3A		Statement of company's objects.	A company may now be a 'general commercial company'. *Ch 4 at 5.2.*
S110 S4	S4	Resolution to alter objects.	Circumstances permitting alteration widened. *Ch 4 at 5.2.*
S111 S30ChA60	S30ChA60	Charitable companies: winding-up.	Minor wording changes only.
S111 SS30A, 30B, 30C ChA60		Alteration of objects clause, invalidity of certain transactions and disclosure of charitable status.	The extent of the reform of the *ultra vires* rule has been restricted for charitable companies. *Ch 4 at 5.7.*
S112		Charitable companies (Scotland).	New provisions dealing with the validity of certain transactions and charitable status.
S113 S381A		Unanimous written resolutions.	New provisions for private companies. *Ch 4 at 2.1.*
S113 S381B		Rights of auditors in relation to written resolution.	Auditors' powers to requisition meetings where a written resolution which concerns them as auditors is proposed. *Ch 4 at 2.1.1.*
S113 S382A		Recording of written resolutions.	New provision. *Ch 4 at 2.1.2.*
S114 Sch15A		Written resolutions of private companies.	Contains the exceptions to the procedure and amends some of the 1985 Act to facilitate the application of written resolutions. *Ch 4 at 2.1.3.*
S115 SS80A, 366A, 369(4), 378(3)		Election by private company to dispense with certain requirements.	May elect to extend the duration of the company's authority to allot shares, dispense with AGMs or accept a lower majority to sanction short notice. *Ch 4 at 2.2.2.*
SS116, 117 S379A		Elective resolution of private company.	New provisions about elective resolutions. *Ch 4 at 2.2.1.*
S118		Introduction: appointment and removal of auditors	
S119 S384		Duty to appoint auditors.	Introduction.
S119 S385	S384(1)-(3)	Appointment at general meeting.	Redrafted to allow for effects of introduction of elective regime.
S119 S385A		Appointment by private company which has elected to dispense with the laying of accounts.	New provision. *Ch 5 at 4.1.1.*

New Section	Old Section	Subject	Extent of change
S119 *S386*		Election by private company to dispense with annual appointment.	New provision. *Ch 5 at 4.1.1.*
S119 *S387*	S384(5)	Appointment by Secretary of State in default of appointment by company.	Redrafted to allow for effects of introduction of elective regime.
S119 *S388*	S384(4) S388(1)(b), (c),2)	Filling of casual vacancies.	Sections reorganised.
S119 *S388A*		Dormant company exempt from obligation to appoint auditors.	Redrafted to allow for effects of introduction of elective regime.
S120 *S389A*	SS237,392, 393	Rights of auditors to information.	
S120 *S390*	S387(1)	Rights of auditors in connection with meetings.	1. Reorganisation of sections; sections dealing with removal of auditors transferred. 2. Rights of auditors to receive information and to require meetings under the elective regime. *Ch 4 at 2.1.1.*
S121 *S390A*	S385	Remuneration of auditors.	1. Redrafted to take account of introduction of elective regime. 2. New disclosures: benefits in kind to be included with remuneration and their nature disclosed (not common practice). *Ch 2 at 2.4.*
S121 *S390B*		Remuneration of auditors for non-audit work.	Secretary of State given the power to introduce by SI this new disclosure requirement. *Ch 2 at 2.4.*
S122 *S391*	SS386,387	Removal of auditors and their rights to attend meetings.	Reorganisation of sections and redrafted to take account of introduction of elective regime.
S122 *S391A*	S388	Rights of auditors who are removed or not reappointed.	Reorganisation of sections.
S122 *S392*	S390	Resignation of auditors.	Minor wording changes only.
S122 *S392A*	S391	Rights of resigning auditors.	Minor wording changes only.
S122 *S393*		Termination of appointment of auditors not appointed annually.	New provision to take account of elective regime. *Ch 5 at 4.1.1.*
S123 *S394*	S390(2)	Statement by persons ceasing to hold office as auditor.	Auditors to make statements about the circumstances of their ceasing to hold office for whatever reason. *Ch 5 at 4.1.2.*

New Section	Old Section	Subject	Extent of change
S124, *S394* *S11(9)* *TULRA74*		Auditors of TUs.	Rights of auditors of corporate TUs.
SS125,126& 127 *SS706,707, 707A, 709, 710,710A &715A*	SS706, 707,709&710	Delivery of documents to the registrar; keeping and inspection of company records and supplementary provisions	1. Existing provisions extended to take account of electronic transmission of information and to take account of company records kept in non-legible form, e.g. microfiche. 2. Definition of 'document' and 'legible'. *Ch 4 at 6.2.*
S128 *S8A*		Form of articles for a partnership company.	New provision. *Ch 4 at 6.7.*
S129 *S23*	S23	Membership of holding company.	1. New exceptions to prohibition. 2. Effect of prior holdings clarified. *Ch 4 at 6.11.*
S130 *SS36,36A, 36B,36C &Sch17*	S36	Company contracts and execution of documents	Abolition of requirement to have a company seal. *Ch 4 at 6.5.*
S131 *S111A*		Members' rights to damages.	Members are no longer prevented from obtaining damages in connection with a share issue purely because they hold shares in the company. *Ch 4 at 6.10.*
S132 *S153(4)(b)*	S153(4)(b)	Financial assistance for the purposes of employees' share scheme.	Any form of financial assistance may now be provided for the purposes of employees' share schemes. *Ch 4 at 6.6.*
S133 *S159A*		Terms and manner of redemption of shares.	Terms of issue must be determined at time of issue. *Ch 4at 6.12.*
S134 *S199(2)*	S199(2)	Disclosure of interests in shares.	Reduction in notifiable interests from 5% to 3%. *Ch 4 at 6.1.*
S134 *SS202(1),(4), 206(8)*	SS202(1), 4), 206(8)	Disclosure of interests in shares.	Reduction in the period for notifying interests from 5 to 2 business days. *Ch 4 at 6.1.*
S134 *S202(3)*	S202(3)	Particulars to be contained in notification.	Particulars must now differentiate between the number of shares and the number of options, convertibles or similar interests. *Ch 4 at 6.1.*
S134 *S210A*		Disclosure of interests in shares.	Power of Secretary of State to make further provision by SI. *Ch 4 at 6.1.*
S135		Restrictions on shares.	New powers to the Secretary of State enabling amendments to be made to provisions relating to orders restricting the rights of shares in some investigations and enquiries into ownership.

New Section	Old Section	Subject	Extent of change
S136 *S287*	S287	A company's registered office.	New provisions dealing with changes in the registered office and the keeping of company registers. *Ch 4 at 6.4.*
S137 *S310*(3)		Insurance for officers and auditors.	Companies are permitted to insure auditors or officers against liability. Directors' report disclosure requirement. *Ch 4 at 6.8.*
S138 *SS332(1)(b), 334,338(4), (6)*	SS332(1)(b), 334,338(4), (6)	Increase of limits for directors' transactions disclosures.	Limits for loans etc. increased. *Ch 4 at 6.9.*
S139 *S363*	SS363-365	Duty to deliver annual returns.	Annual returns must now be delivered not later than the company's 'return date'. *Ch 4 at 4.1.*
S139 *S364*		Contents of annual return.	Existing requirements as to content have been relaxed but certain new disclosures required. *Ch 4 at 4.2.*
S139 *S364A*		Contents of annual return: particulars of share capital and shareholders.	Certain existing disclosures are no longer required. *Ch 4 at 4.3.*
S139 *S365*		Annual returns: supplementary.	Secretary of State may, by SI, amend or repeal provisions on information to be disclosed. *Ch 4 at 4.3.*
S140 *SS463(1)& 464*	SS463(1)& 464	Floating charges (Scotland).	1. Date when charge attaches. 2. Ranking of charges. 3. The maximum amount of floating charges securing contingent liabilities defined for the purposes of subsequent floating charges. *Ch 8 at 3.2.*
S141 *S651*	S651	Power of court to declare dissolution of company void.	Indefinite time limit to restore struck-off company to pursue personal or fatal injuries claim. *Ch 8 at 3.1.*
S142 *S711A*		Abolition of doctrine of deemed notice.	With exceptions, the doctrine of deemed notice has been abolished. *Ch 4 at 6.3.*
S143 *S723A*		Rights of inspection of registers.	Minor wording changes to many sections of the 1985 Act. New power of Secretary of State to make regulations regarding the availability of registers for inspection. *Ch 4 at 3.3.*
S144& Sch18 *SS736-736B*	S736	'Subsidiary', 'holding company' and 'wholly-owned subsidiary';consequential amendments and savings.	1. New definitions and supplementary provisions. *Ch 3 at 2.1, 2.3 and 2.4.* 2. modifies other legislation referring to these terms. *Ch 3 at 2.4.*
S145& Sch19		Minor amendments of the 1985 Act	

New Section	Old Section	Subject	Extent of change
8Sch19 *SS459(1), 460(1)(b)*	SS459(1), 460(1)(b)	Protection of company's members against unfair prejudice	Sections now also apply to actions unfairly prejudicial to the interests of all members of a company, not 'some part of its members', as previously. *Ch 4 at 6.10.*

Part VI

New Section	Old Section	Subject	Extent of change
S146 *S75A-F FTA73*		Voluntary pre-notification procedure.	New procedures under which merger references may be avoided. *Ch 6 at 2.*
S147 *SS75G-75K FTA73*		Undertakings as alternative to merger reference.	New provisions. *Ch 6 at 3.*
S148 *S93A FTA73*		Enforcement of undertakings.	New provisions. *Ch 6 at 3.4.*
S149 *S75(4A)-(4M)FTA73*		Temporary restrictions on share dealing.	Parties to a merger are prohibited from acquiring each other's shares, except with the consent of the Secretary of State, from the time the merger is referred to the MMC. *Ch 6 at 4.*
S150 *S66A FTA73*		Obtaining control by stages.	New provisions. *Ch 6 at 5.*
S151 *S93B FTA73*		False or misleading information.	New offences. *Ch 6 at 6.*
S152		Fees	Power to levy fees granted. *Ch 6 at 7.*
S153& Sch 20		Mergers and related matters.	Minor amendments to the competition legislation.

Part VII

New Section	Old Section	Subject	Extent of change
SS154-191& Sch21&22			New legislation dealing with insolvent persons operating in financial markets. *Ch 8 at 1 and 2 .*

Part VIII

New Section	Old Section	Subject	Extent of change
S192 *SS47A, 47B FSA86*		Statements of principle.	New provision. *Ch 9 at 2.1.*
S193 *S62A,22A Sch 11FSA86*		Right to bring actions for breach of rules and regulations.	Action can now only be brought by a private investor. *Ch 9 at 3.*
S194 *SS63A, 63B FSA86*		Designated rules and regulations.	Application of designated rules and regulations to members of SROs, their modification and waiver. *Ch 9 at 2.2.*
S195 *S63C FSA86*		Codes of practice.	New provision. *Ch 9 at 2.3.*

New Section	Old Section	Subject	Extent of change
S196 *S128A FSA86*		Relations with other regulatory authorities.	SIB may take account of the rules of another regulatory body when considering the recognition of a SRO or RPB. *Ch 9 at 5.1.*
S196 *S128B FSA86*		Relations with other regulatory authorities.	Clarification of the extent to which the SIB may rely on other regulatory bodies. *Ch 9 at 5.2.*
S196 *S128CFSA86*		Relations with other regulators.	New provisions concerning reciprocity in dealings with overseas regulators. *Ch 9 at 5.3.*
S197 *SS150(6), 154(5)FSA86*	*SS150(6), 154(5)FSA86*	Exclusion of liability in respect of false or misleading listing particulars.	Clarifying provision.
SS198,199, SS160A, 170(2)- (4)FSA86	*SS170(2)-(4), FSA86*	Offers of unlisted securities; offers of securities by private companies and old public companies.	Wider power to exempt investment advertisments. *Ch 9 at 7.1.1.*
S200 *S188 FSA86*	*S188 FSA86*	Jurisdiction of High Court and Court of Session.	Proceedings may now be brought against a recognised SRO in any part of the UK. *Ch 9 at 7.2.*
S201 *S192FSA86*	*S192FSA86*	Directions to secure compliance with international obligations.	Directions may now also be given to RIEs and RCHs. *Ch 9 at 6.*
S202 *S195FSA86*	*S195FSA86*	Offers of short-dated debentures	Offer of debentures repayable within 5 years (previously one year) not to be treated as an offer to the public. *Ch 9 at 7.1.2.*
S203 *3Sch 2,3Sch3 FSA86*	*3Sch 2,3Sch3 FSA86*	Standard of protection for investors.	Amends the existing criteria. *Ch 9 at 2.4.*
S204 *3ASch 2, 3ASch3, 2ASch7 FSA86*		Costs of compliance.	New provisions: costs imposed on investment businesses must be no more than those necessary to achieve adequate investor protection. *Ch 9 at 4.*
S205 *6Sch4FSA86*		Requirements for recognition of investment exchange.	Clarification. *Ch 9 at 7.3.*
S206& Sch23		Consequential amendments of the FSA86.	

Part IX

S207		Transfer of securities.	New power to introduce SI enabling title to securities to be evidenced and transferred without a written instrument. Minor in effect.

New Section	Old Section	Subject	Extent of change
Part X			
S208 *S21(4) CDDA86*		Offences in connection with disqualification of directors.	New provisions dealing with summary proceedings in Scotland. *Ch 8 at 3.3.*
S209 *S8CS(ID)A85*	S8CS(ID)A85	Prosecutions in connection with insider dealing.	Minor wording changes only.
S210l *4Sch3PPA75*	4Sch3PPA75	Duty of insurance companies to supply statements of premium income.	Statements in respect of the preceding year need only be sent to the Secretary of State if requested.
S211 *Sch15BSA86*	Sch 15BSA86	Application of companies winding-up legislation.	Minor wording changes only.
S211 *S22A CDDA86*		Application of CDDA86 to building societies.	Replaces provisions.
S212& Sch 24		Repeals.	
SS213&214		Northern Ireland.	Application of Act to Northern Ireland. *Ch 1 at 2.*
S215		Commencement & transitional provisions.	To be introduced at varying dates by SI.
S216		Citation of Act.	

Formats

The Act does not include full formats for group accounts; instead, those items (for example minority interests) that are needed to cover the requirements of consolidated group accounts have been added to the existing formats for individual companies. No items have been removed from the individual company formats. As a result, the formats applicable to group companies include items (for example, 'shares in group undertakings') which will not normally appear in consolidated accounts.

The individual company formats have themselves been revised to take account of the new terminology relating to subsidiary and associated undertakings.

Balance sheet format 1

A   Called up share capital not paid
B   Fixed assets
     I   Intangible assets
           1   Development costs
           2   Concessions, patents, licences, trade marks and similar rights and assets
           3   Goodwill
           4   Payments on account
     II   Tangible assets
           1   Land and buildings
           2   Plant and machinery
           3   Fixtures, fittings, tools and equipment
           4   Payments on account and assets in course of construction
     III   Investments
           1   Shares in group undertakings
           2   Loans to group undertakings
           3   (a)   Interests in associated undertakings   )[1&2]
                     (b)   Other participating interests   )
           4   Loans to undertakings in which the company has a participating interest[2]
           5   Other investments other than loans
           6   Other loans
           7   Own shares

C   Current assets
    I   Stocks
             1   Raw materials and consumables
             2   Work in progress
             3   Finished goods and goods for resale
             4   Payments on account
    II   Debtors
             1   Trade debtors
             2   Amount owed by group undertakings
             3   Amount owed by undertakings in which the company has a participating interest[2]
             4   Other debtors
             5   Called up share capital not paid
             6   Prepayments and accrued income
    III   Investments
             1   Shares in group undertakings
             2   Own shares
              3   Other investments
    IV   Cash at bank and in hand
D   Prepayments and accrued income
E   Creditors: amounts falling due within one year
             1   Debenture loans
             2   Bank loans and overdrafts
             3   Payments received on account
             4   Trade creditors
             5   Bills of exchange payable
              6   Amounts owed to group undertakings
             7   Amounts owed to undertakings in which the company has a participating interest[2]
             8   Other creditors including taxation and social security
             9   Accruals and deferred income
F   Net current assets (liabilities)
G   Total assets less current liabilities
H   Creditors: amounts falling due after more than one year
             1   Debenture loans
             2   Bank loans and overdrafts
             3   Payments received on account
             4   Trade creditors
             5   Bills of exchange payable
              6   Amounts owed to group undertakings
             7   Amounts owed to undertakings in which the company has a participating interest[2]
             8   Other creditors including taxation and social security
             9   Accruals and deferred income
I   Provision for liabilities and charges
             1   Pensions and similar obligations
             2   Taxation, including deferred taxation
             3   Other provisions
J   Accruals and deferred income
*   Minority interests[3]

K   Capital and reserves
    I   Called up share capital
    II   Share premium account
    III   Revaluation reserve
    IV   Other reserves
           1   Capital redemption reserve
           2   Reserve for own shares
           3   Reserves provided for by the articles of association
           4   Other reserves
    V   Profit and loss account
*   Minority interests [3]

Balance sheet format 2

ASSETS
A   Called up share capital not paid
B   Fixed assets
    I   Intangible assets
           1   Development costs
           2   Concessions, patents, licences, trade marks and similar rights and assets
           3   Goodwill
           4   Payments on account
    II   Tangible assets
           1   Land and buildings
           2   Plant and machinery
           3   Fixtures, fittings, tools and equipment
           4   Payments on account and assets in course of construction
    III   Investments
           1   Shares in group undertakings
           2   Loans to group undertakings
           3   (a)   Interests in associated undertakings   )[1&2]
                (b)   Other participating interests   )
           4   Loans to undertakings in which the company has a participating interest[2]
           5   Other investments other than loans
           6   Other loans
           7   Own shares
C   Current assets
    I   Stocks
           1   Raw materials and consumables
           2   Work in progress
           3   Finished goods and goods for resale
           4   Payments on account
    II   Debtors
           1   Trade debtors
           2   Amount owed by group undertakings
           3   Amount owed by undertakings in which the company has a participating interest[2]
           4   Other debtors
           5   Called up share capital not paid
           6   Prepayments and accrued income

III   Investments
     1   Shares in group undertakings
     2   Own shares
     3   Other investments
IV   Cash at bank and in hand

D   Prepayments and accrued income

LIABILITIES

A   Capital and reserves
    I   Called up share capital
    II   Share premium account
    III   Revaluation reserve
    IV   Other reserves
        1   Capital redemption reserve
        2   Reserve for own shares
        3   Reserves provided for by the articles of association
        4   Other reserves
    V   Profit and loss account

*   Minority interests [3]

B   Provision for liabilities and charges
        1   Pensions and similar obligations
        2   Taxation, including deferred taxation
        3   Other provisions

C   Creditors
        1   Debenture loans
        2   Bank loans and overdrafts
        3   Payments received on account
        4   Trade creditors
        5   Bills of exchange payable
        6   Amounts owed to group undertakings
        7   Amounts owed to undertakings in which the company has a participating interest[2]
        8   Other creditors including taxation and social security
        9   Accruals and deferred income

D   Accruals and deferred income

Profit and loss account format 1

1   Turnover
2   Cost of sales
3   Gross profit
4   Distribution costs
5   Administrative expenses
6   Other operating income
7   Income from shares in group undertakings
8   (a)   Income from interests in associated undertakings   )[2&4]
     (b)   Income from other participating interests   )
9   Income from other fixed asset investments
10   Other interest receivable and similar income
11   Amounts written off investments
12   Interest payable and similar charges

13   Tax on profit or loss on ordinary activities
14   Profit or loss on ordinary activities after taxation
*   Minority interests[3]
15   Extraordinary income
16   Extraordinary charges
17   Extraordinary profit or loss
18   Tax on extraordinary profit or loss
*   Minority interests[3]
19   Other taxes not shown under the above items
20   Profit or loss for the financial year

Profit and loss account format 2

1   Turnover
2   Change in stocks of finished goods and in work in progress
3   Own work capitalised
4   Other operating income
5   (a)   Raw materials and consumables
      (b)   Other external charges
6   Staff costs:
      (a)   Wages and salaries
      (b)   Social security costs
      (c)   Other pension costs
7   (a)   Depreciation and other amounts written off tangible and intangible fixed assets
      (b)   Exceptional amounts written off current assets
8   Other operating charges
9   Income from shares in group undertakings
10   (a)   Income from interests in associated undertakings   )[2&4]
       (b)   Income from other participating interests   )
11   Income from other fixed asset investments
12   Other interest receivable and similar income
13   Amounts written off investments
14   Interest payable and similar charges
15   Tax on profit or loss on ordinary activities
16   Profit or loss on ordinary activities after taxation
*   Minority interests[3]
17   Extraordinary income
18   Extraordinary charges
19   Extraordinary profit or loss
20   Tax on extraordinary profit or loss
*   Minority interests[3]
21   Other taxes not shown under the above items
22   Profit or loss for the financial year

Profit and loss account format 3

A Charges
1   Cost of sales
2   Distribution costs
3   Administrative expenses

4   Amounts written off investments
5   Interest payable and similar charges
6   Tax on profit or loss on ordinary activities
7   Profit or loss on ordinary activities after taxation
*   Minority interests[3]
8   Extraordinary charges
9   Tax on extraordinary profit or loss
*   Minority interests[3]
10   Other taxes not shown under the above items
11   Profit or loss for the financial year
B   Income
1   Turnover
2   Other operating income
3   Income from shares in group undertakings
4   (a)   Income from interests in associated undertakings   )[2&4]
        (b)   Income from other participating interests   )
5   Income from other fixed asset investments
6   Other interest receivable and similar income
7   Profit or loss on ordinary activities after taxation
*   Minority interests[3]
8   Extraordinary income
*   Minority interests[3]
9   Profit or loss for the financial year

Profit and loss account format 4

A   Charges
1   Reduction in stocks of finished goods and in work in progress
2   (a) Raw materials and consumables
        (b) Other external charges
3   Staff costs:
        (a)   Wages and salaries
        (b)   Social security costs
        (c)   Other pension costs
4   (a)   Depreciation and other amounts written off tangible and intangible fixed assets
        (b)   Exceptional amounts written off current assets
5   Other operating charges
6   Amounts written off investments
7   Interest payable and similar charges
8   Tax on profit or loss on ordinary activities
9   Profit or loss on ordinary activities after taxation
*   Minority interests[3]
10   Extraordinary charges
11   Tax on extraordinary profit or loss
*   Minority interests[3]
12   Other taxes not shown under the above items
13   Profit or loss for the financial year
B   Income
1   Turnover

2	Increase in stocks of finished goods and in work in progress	
3	Own work capitalised	
4	Other operating income	
5	Income from shares in group undertakings	
6	(a) Income from interests in associated undertakings	)2&4
	(b) Income from other participating interests	)
7	Income from other fixed asset investments	
8	Other interest receivable and similar income	
9	Profit or loss on ordinary activities after taxation	
*	Minority interests[3]	
10	Extraordinary income	
*	Minority interests[3]	
11	Profit or loss for the financial year	

Notes

1   For individual company balance sheets, these two lines are combined and shown as 'Participating interests'.

2   For group accounts, section 22 of the Act (section 260(7)CA85 as revised), 'participating interests' include interests of all group companies. See Chapter 3 at 2.5.

3   'Minority interests' has not been allocated a reference. It is to be treated as an item with an Alphabetic or Roman reference in the balance sheet and an Arabic reference in the profit and loss account. There are two alternative balance sheet positions; minority interests may either be deducted from net assets or included in shareholders' funds. There are alternative positions in the profit and loss account formats 3 and 4, depending on whether the minority shares in a profit or loss. Provision is made in all profit and loss account formats for the minority's share in extraordinary items.

4   For individual company profit and loss accounts, these two lines are combined and shown as 'Income from participating interests'

Small and medium-sized groups

This Appendix gives a series of examples intended to illustrate the operation of the rules in section 13 of the Act which provides that small and medium-sized groups need not prepare consolidated accounts.

Section 13(1) of the Act inserts a new section 249 into the 1985 Act. Under new section 249(3), status as a small or medium-sized group depends on the satisfaction of two out of the following three criteria:

1.	Aggregate turnover	Not more than £8 million net (or £9.6 million gross)
2.	Aggregate balance sheet total	Not more than £3.9 million net (or £4.7 million gross)
3.	Aggregate number of employees	Not more than 250.

The meaning of 'gross' and 'net' is explained in Chapter 3 at 3.1.1.

It should be borne in mind that the interpretations of the rules adopted in the examples may not be the only interpretations which emerge.

Example A   Small and medium-sized groups

P Limited has just one subsidiary undertaking, S Limited. Both companies have an accounting reference date of December 31. The accounting reference periods are shortened to September 30 in 1992 and the following information is taken from the statutory accounts of the two companies:

Accounting reference date	Turnover	Balance sheet total	Number of employees
	£m	£m	
P Limited			
December 31, 1989	4.7	2.5	125
December 31, 1990	5.0	2.5	135
December 31, 1991	5.5	2.7	140
December 31, 1992	4.5	2.4	140
S Limited			
December 31, 1989	5.0	2.3	100
December 31, 1990	5.1	2.2	105
December 31, 1991	5.25	2.2	115
December 31, 1992	4.5	2.4	120

No trading has taken place between the two companies and consequently there are no intercompany balances included in the balance sheet totals and no intercompany sales in turnover. P acquired S for £1,000,000 and this cost is reflected in each of the balance sheet totals of P shown above. In which financial years, if any, will the P group be exempt from preparing consolidated accounts as a small or medium-sized group?

Financial year ended December 31, 1990:

The group will qualify for exemption if it satisfies two out of the three criteria for the financial years ended December 31, 1989 and 1990 (see new section 249(1)(b) in the boxed extract below.)

Extract : Small and medium-sized groups
249. — (1) A group qualifies as small or medium-sized in relation to a financial year if the qualifying conditions are met—
(a) in the case of the parent company's first financial year, in that year, and
(b) in the case of any subsequent financial year, in that year and the preceding year.
(2) A group shall be treated as qualifying as small or medium-sized in relation to a financial year—
(a) if it so qualified in relation to the previous financial year under subsection (1);or
(b) if it was treated as so qualifying in relation to the previous year by virtue of paragraph (a) and the qualifying conditions are met in the year in question.

New section 249(2)(a) does not apply because the group could not have qualified or been treated as qualifying in the previous financial year as this is the first year to which the new exemption applies). Aggregating the figures from the statutory accounts of the two companies gives the following results:

	Gross basis	Net basis
Financial year ended December 31, 1989:		
Turnover	£9.7m	£9.7m
Balance sheet total	£4.8m	£3.8m
Number of employees	225	225
Financial year ended December 31, 1990:		
Turnover	£10.1m	£10.1m
Balance sheet total	£4.7m	£3.7m
Number of employees	240	240

For the year ended December 31, 1989, the third limit is satisfied and the second limit is satisfied on a net basis. For the year ended December 31, 1990, the third limit is satisfied and so is the second (on either basis). The P group will therefore be exempt from preparing consolidated accounts for the year ended December 31, 1990.

The foregoing assumes that this is the first year to which the new exemption applies. It is possible that the commencement order implementing the exemption will contain transitional provisions affecting this example, which assumes that there will be no such provisions.

Financial year ended December 31, 1991:

Aggregating the figures from the statutory accounts of the two companies gives the following results in relation to the financial year ended December 31, 1991:

	Gross basis	Net basis
Turnover	£10.75m	£10.75m
Balance sheet total	£4.9m	£3.9m
Number of employees	255	255

The only limit satisfied is the second one on a net basis so the group does not satisfy two out of three limits for the financial year ended December 31, 1991. It will nevertheless be exempt from preparing consolidated accounts by virtue of new section 249(2)(a) (see the boxed extract above).

Financial year ended September 30, 1992:

Aggregating the figures from the statutory accounts of the two companies gives the following results in relation to the financial year ended September 30, 1992:

	Gross basis	Net basis
Turnover	£9m	£9m
Balance sheet total	£4.8m	£3.8m
Number of employees	260	260

No adjustment is made in respect of the short accounting reference period (see Chapter 3 at 3.1.1) so the first limit is satisfied on a gross basis, the second on a net basis and the third is not satisfied. This means that two out of the three criteria are satisfied in relation to the financial year ended September 30, 1992 (as noted in Chapter 3 at 3.1.1, the bases can apparently be mixed). P will therefore be exempt from preparing consolidated accounts by virtue of new section 249(2)(b) (see the boxed extract above).

In the above example, the shortening of the accounting reference period in 1992 had the effect of making the exemption available in circumstances where it would have been unlikely to have applied had the accounting reference period not been shortened. Conversely, an extension of an accounting reference period can result in consolidated accounts having to be prepared in circumstances where they would not have been required had the period not been extended. Also, no adjustments are made when companies within a group have accounting reference periods of different lengths.

Changes in group structure are ignored when deciding whether the limits are exceeded for a particular financial year and the one preceding it but are otherwise taken into account in determining a group's status. The position can differ depending on whether a company already has subsidiary undertakings when it acquires a new subsidiary undertaking, as is shown by Examples B and C.

Example B   Small and medium-sized groups and change in group structure

A Limited acquired its only subsidiary undertaking, B Limited, on January 1, 1992. A has an accounting reference date of December 31 and B of March 31. B shortens its accounting reference period ending March 31, 1993 to end on December 31, 1992. The following figures are taken from the statutory accounts of the two companies:

Accounting reference date	Turnover £m	Balance sheet total £m	Number of employees
A Limited			
December 31,1991	7.0	2.0	150
December 31,1992	7.5	2.2	170
B Limited			
December 31,1991	2.5	1.0	70
December 31,1992	2.7	1.2	75
December 31,1992	2.5	1.5	90

No trading has taken place between the two companies and consequently there are no intercompany balances included in the balance sheet totals and no intercompany sales in turnover. A acquired B for £500,000 and this cost is reflected in the balance sheet total of A as at December 31, 1992.

Is the A group entitled to exemption from preparing consolidated accounts for the financial year ended December 31, 1992?

The group will qualify if it satisfied two of the three criteria for the financial years ended December 31, 1991 and 1992 (new section 249(1)(b) — see the boxed extract in Example A above). Note that new section 249(2) does not apply because the group could not have qualified or been treated as qualifying in the previous year because it did not exist. The figures to be aggregated for B are in each case those for its financial year ended with or last before that of A (new section 249(5))— i.e. in relation to 1991, March 31, 1991 and in relation to 1992, December 31, 1992. This produces the following results:

	Gross basis	Net basis
December 31, 1991:		
Turnover	£9.5m	£9.5m
Balance sheet total	£3m	£2.5m
Number of employees	220	220
December 31, 1992:		
Turnover	£10m	£10m
Balance sheet total	£3.7m	£3.2m
Number of employees	260	260

In 1991, all three limits are satisfied on a gross basis but in 1992 only the second limit is satisfied. A must therefore prepare group accounts for the year ended December 31, 1992.

Example C   *Small and medium-sized groups and change in structure of pre-existing group*

The facts are as in Example B except that A has owned D Limited for many years. D Limited does not affect the question of whether two out of the three criteria are satisfied in relation to the financial years ended December 31, 1991 and 1992. The A group was exempt from preparing group accounts for the year ended December 31, 1991 by virtue of satisfying two of the three criteria in both that year and the preceding year.

Is the A group entitled to exemption from preparing consolidated accounts for the financial year ended December 31, 1992?

As in Example B, the A group does not satisfy two out of the three criteria for the financial year ended December 31, 1992 and therefore does not qualify under new section 249(1)(b). However, this time the group did exist in the previous year so its status in that year is relevant. The A group is therefore exempt from preparing consolidated accounts by virtue of its qualification under new section 249 (1)(b) for the financial year ended December 31, 1991 — (new section 249(2)(a) — see the boxed extract in Example A above).

In Example B, figures for B were relevant for its financial year ended March 31, 1991 even though it was not acquired until 1992. The example also shows that, when a parent company has a longer accounting reference period than a subsidiary undertaking, the figures for a particular accounting reference period of the subsidiary undertaking are sometimes left out of account in deciding whether the criteria are satisfied. Conversely, when a parent company has a shorter accounting reference period than a subsidiary undertaking, the figures for a particular accounting reference period of the subsidiary undertaking are sometimes taken into account twice in deciding whether the criteria are satisfied.

The introduction of a new parent company for a group can affect its entitlement to exemption as is shown by the following example.

Example D   Effect of introduction of new parent company

The facts are as in Example A, except that on January 1, 1991 N Limited becomes the parent company of P. N is a new company formed purely for the purpose of becoming the parent company of the group so its only asset is its investment in P and for the entire period from its incorporation to December 31, 1991 it has no turnover and no employees. It has an accounting reference date of December 31.

Is the N group entitled to exemption from preparing consolidated accounts for the financial year ended December 31, 1991?

Since this is its first accounting reference period, N can only claim exemption if two out of the three criteria are satisfied for the year ended December 31, 1991 (new section 249(1)(a) — see the boxed extract in Example A above).

This gives the following results:

	Gross and net basis
Turnover	£10.75m
Number of employees	255

Both of these limits are exceeded so two out of the three criteria are not satisfied and N cannot claim exemption. Had N not been introduced as the new holding company, the P group would have been exempt as is shown by Example A.

As a result of the above, two points are worth noting:

(a)   in this example, the introduction of a new parent company had the effect that the group became unable to claim exemption in a year when exemption would have been available had the new parent company not been introduced. This happened because, if it is the first accounting reference period of the parent company, the satisfaction of two out of the three criteria only in that year is relevant. Therefore the fact that the group was entitled to exemption in the previous year (1990) because it satisfied two out of the three criteria for 1989 and 1990 no longer has any bearing on the position for the financial year ended December 31,1991. In other circumstances, the introduction of a new holding company could have precisely the opposite effect. For example, this would happen if two out of the three criteria were satisfied for the first accounting reference period of the new company but the group had not been entitled to exemption and did not satisfy two out of the three criteria in the previous year; and

(b)   in 1991, although the N group is not entitled to exemption, the P sub-group is exempt. As noted in (a), the reverse could be true with the N group being exempt but the P sub-group not exempt. In those circumstances, if N took advantage of the exemption, the P sub-group would have to file consolidated accounts. If, however N chose to prepare consolidated accounts, P could claim exemption as an intermediate parent company (see Chapter 3 at 3.1.2).

ALSO AVAILABLE ...

UK GAAP: Generally Accepted Accounting Practice in the United Kingdom

Written by the Technical Department of Ernst & Young; principal authors and editors: Mike Davies, Ron Paterson and Allister Wilson; 1,044 pages.

Price £24.50, available from all major bookshops.

ISBN 0 85121 4851